DESPERATE DAN
SEAVIEW HOTEL
PHEW! WHAT A JOB WRITING ALL THESE HOLIDAY POSTCARDS!
MUST DASH TO THE BEACH AND COOL OFF WITH A SWIM. AH! THERE'S A POST BOX.
I FORGOT TO STAMP THEM!
WHAT'LL I DO? BETTER NOT BUST THE POST BOX OPEN! I KNOW! I'LL BLOW 'EM BACK OUT THROUGH THE SLOT.
ROAD
I'LL BORROW A LENGTH OF THAT GASPIPE.
JUST BEND THE END OF THE PIPE, SO—
NOW PUSH THE PIPE INTO THE SLOT TILL THE BENT END IS AT THE BOTTOM.
THEN BLOW— OH, DRAT! I'VE BLOWN TOO HARD!
BLAST
NOW I'LL HAVE TO WASTE TEN MINUTES WAITING FOR EVERYTHING TO COME DOWN!
TEN MINUTES LATER—
THAT'S ABOUT THE LOT, I THINK.
WELL, DOGGONE! I CLEAN FORGOT ABOUT THE LID!
CLANG
SAY! PULL IT HARD DOWN AND THAT'LL MAKE A GOOD HAT!
IT SURE KEEPS THE SUN OFF!
GUESS I'LL POST MY CARDS LATER. IT'S TOO WARM TO GO LOOKING FOR A POST OFFICE!
THERE SURE IS SOMETHING MIGHTY FAMILIAR ABOUT DAN'S HAT!
GPO
HA-HA! LOOK AT DAN'S MEXICAN SOMBRERO! IT'S MADE OF SOLID IRON!

DINAH MO
HERE — GET SOMETHING FOR YOURSELF OFF THE ICE-CREAM VAN, MO!
DING — DONG!
ICES
THANKS, DAD!
THINK I'LL HAVE A SUPER-DUPER, GIANT CORNET!
ZIP!
BAH! THE VAN'S GONE ROUND THE CORNER — I'LL NEVER CATCH IT . . .
SKID!
. . . UNLESS I TAKE A SHORT CUT!
ANOTHER FENCE . . .
ZOOM!
. . . BUT IT WON'T STOP ME!
SNAP!
THUD!
HOI!
CRASH!
YIKES!
THUMP!
COME BACK HERE!
I CAN STILL CATCH THE VAN UNLESS MR LEE CATCHES ME FIRST!
AH, THERE IT IS!
DING-DONG!
GIVE ME A LIFT AND I'LL GIVE YER A LICK OF MY ICE-CREAM, JOE!
ER — OKAY!
FASTER — FASTER!
DING-DONG!
DAN 29.11.86

MY LIFT'S CRASHED, BUT THIS CARTIE'S GOIN' MY WAY!
HELP!
EH?
HEY! COME BACK WIV ME CARTIE!
YOU'LL GET IT BACK— PLUS A LICK OF MY ICE-CREAM!
OUT OF MY WAY!
WOW!
THUD!
GET HER!
I'LL BORROW YER SKATEBOARD FOR A LICK OF MY ICE!
PHEW! I'VE CAUGHT THE VAN AT LAST!
OSL 176Y
YOW! HOO, BOY! DID I CATCH IT?
WAP!
OSL Y
ONE SUPER-DUPER, GIANT CORNET, PLEASE!
YOU'LL BE LUCKY...
...YOU'VE BEEN FOLLOWIN' THE WRONG VAN!
GORDON SMITH PLUMBER
OH, NO!
GUESS WHO'S GONNA GET A LICKIN' NOW...
...MO— WHEN WE GET HOLD OF HER!
HELP!

BERYL the PERIL
I'M GOING RIDING, FOLKS.
MIGHT BE A BIT HARD TO GET MOUNTED THOUGH.
I'LL JUST HAVE T'TAKE STEPS TO GET MOUNTED.
OH, VERY FUNNEE!
CRASH!
SNIGGER.
Soon —
GIVEN UP TRYING TO RIDE THAT HORSE?
ME?
DON'T BE DAFT, READER . . .
. . . THE HORSE HASN'T BEEN BORN . . .
. . . THAT CAN GET THE BETTER OF THE PERIL!
FLOP!
NEIGH!

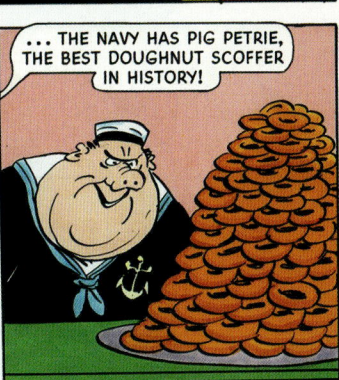

CORPORAL CLOTT

Panel 1: CLOTT. WHAT'S YOUR FAVOURITE FOOD? QUICK NOW! NO TIME FOR THOUGHT! — J-JELLIED EE-EELS, S-SIR!

Panel 2: GOOD! YOUR OUR ENTRANT FOR THIS! *WE WANT YOUR MOUTH! FORCES EATING COMPETITION* — THANK YOU, SIR.

Panel 3: Next day — the contest! YOUR OPPONENTS ARE ALREADY IN THE CANTEEN, CLOTT! — I'M READY, SIR.

Panel 4: OH, NO! IT CAN'T BE...

Panel 5: ...THE NAVY HAS PIG PETRIE, THE BEST DOUGHNUT SCOFFER IN HISTORY!

Panel 6: AND THE AIR FORCE HAS HIPPO HUGHES — THE SPAGHETTI SPECIALIST.

Panel 7: THOSE TWO ARE LEGENDS! I'LL NEVER BEAT THEM! — AND REPRESENTING THE ARMY IS CORPORAL CLOTT WHO SPECIALISES IN...

Panel 8: WHISPER-WHISPER MUTTER-MUTTER... AHEM! YES-YES!

Panel 9: CORPORAL CLOTT IS OFF TO GET HIS NOSH!

Panel 10: Seconds later— CORPORAL CLOTT SPECIALISES IN...

Panel 11: EELS! THEY'RE ALIVE! YEUCH!

Panel 12: I FEEL SICK! ME TOO! THE WINNER — CORPORAL CLOTT!

Panel 13: I WASN'T GOING TO TELL THEM IT WAS ONLY JELLIED EELS I LIKE! *EATING CHAMPION 1988*

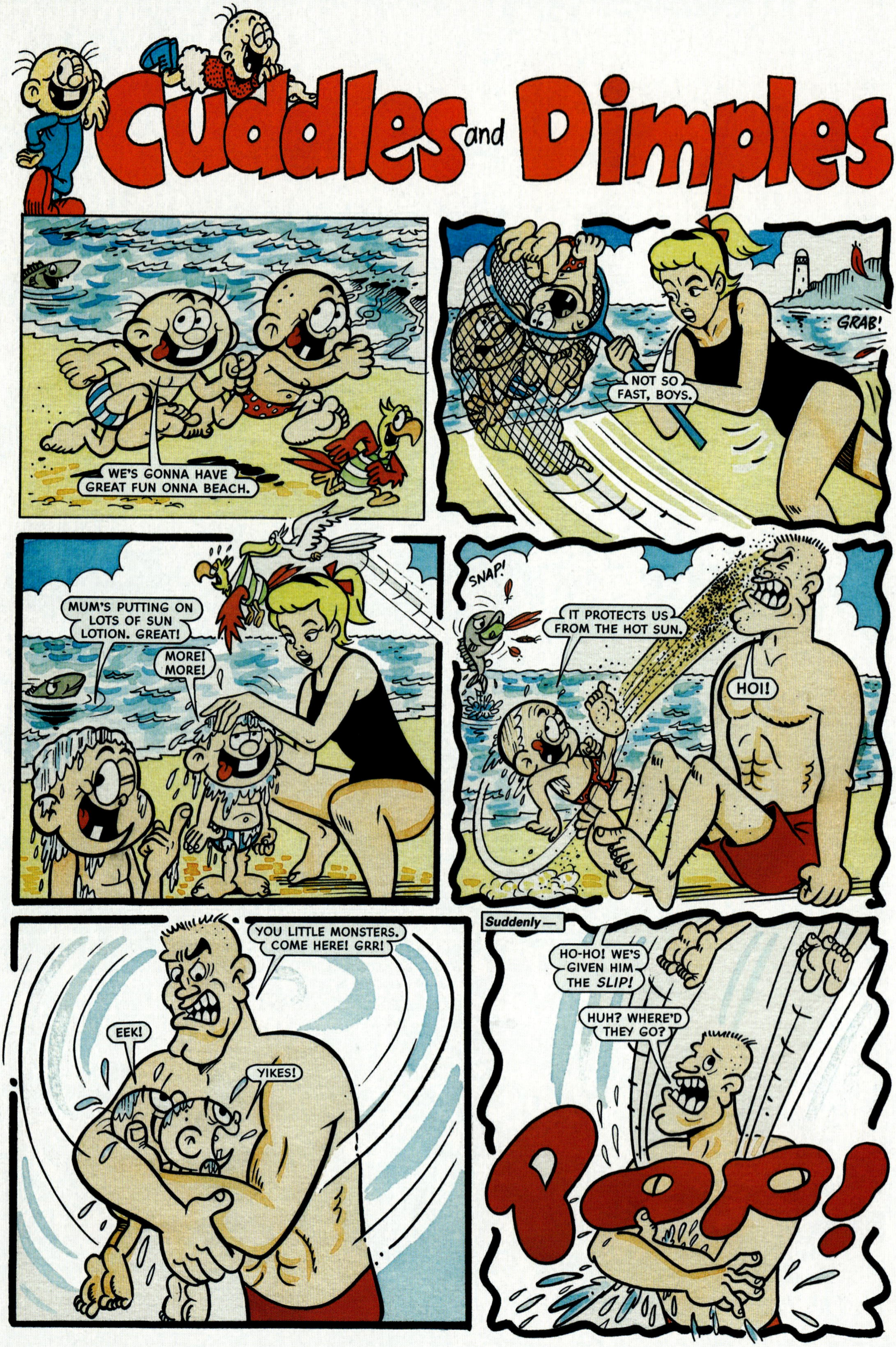
Cuddles and Dimples
WE'S GONNA HAVE GREAT FUN ONNA BEACH.
NOT SO FAST, BOYS.
GRAB!
MUM'S PUTTING ON LOTS OF SUN LOTION. GREAT!
MORE! MORE!
SNAP!
IT PROTECTS US FROM THE HOT SUN.
HOI!
YOU LITTLE MONSTERS. COME HERE! GRR!
EEK!
YIKES!
Suddenly—
HO-HO! WE'S GIVEN HIM THE SLIP!
HUH? WHERE'D THEY GO?
POP!

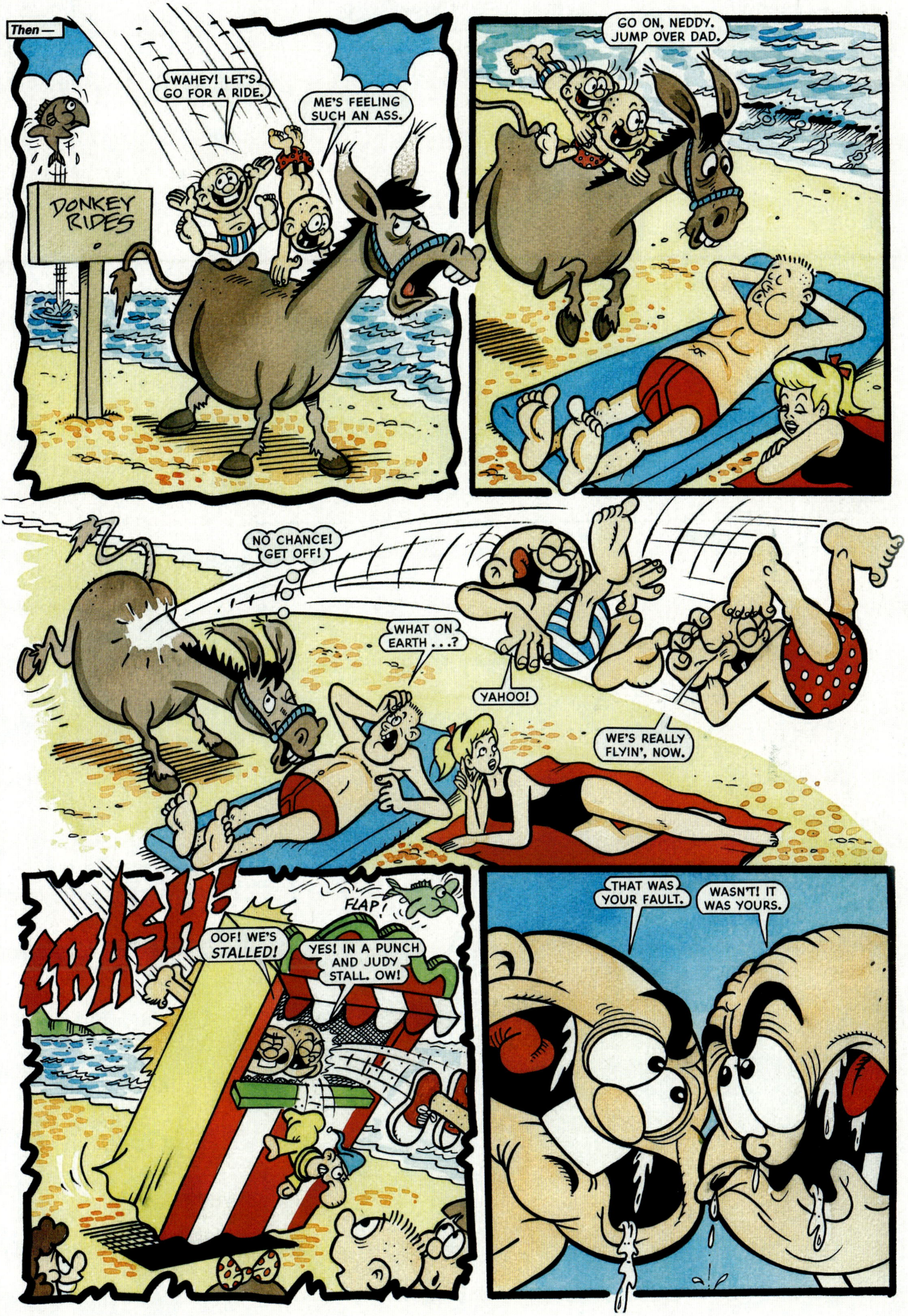Then—
WAHEY! LET'S GO FOR A RIDE.
ME'S FEELING SUCH AN ASS.
DONKEY RIDES
GO ON, NEDDY. JUMP OVER DAD.
NO CHANCE! GET OFF!
WHAT ON EARTH . . .?
YAHOO!
WE'S REALLY FLYIN', NOW.
CRASH!
FLAP!
OOF! WE'S STALLED!
YES! IN A PUNCH AND JUDY STALL. OW!
THAT WAS YOUR FAULT.
WASN'T! IT WAS YOURS.

BOOT!
TAKE THAT!
BASH!
OOYAH! YOU TAKE THIS.
BAH! THE KIDS WOULD RATHER WATCH THEM THAN ME.
BOP!
THAT'S THE WAY TO DO IT!
GO ON! PUNCH HIM AGAIN.
SMASHING STUFF!

Advertisement

PLAY EPIC GAMES!

PET PANIC!

BR?IN F?RT

LITTLE MENACE'S GREAT ESCAPE GAME

Betty & the Yeti's UNICORN GAME

TUNNEL TROUBLE

BIG BEANO TRIVIA QUIZ

Big Eggo's ANGRY GOOSE GAME

GO TO **BEANO.COM/ARCADE**

or scan me!

HYDE & SHRIEK

TIME FOR BREKKIE!

YANK! DONG! BONG!

SQUONK!

Abandon hope all ye who slumber here!

BUT — YOU'LL HAVE TO FETCH YOUR OWN BREAKFAST — I'M DUE MY 2 DAYS' ANNUAL LEAVE!

Butling Contract

GASP! TWO DAYS' HOLIDAY? WHAT'LL I DO WHILE YOU'RE AWAY?

FRANKLY, YOUNG MASTER — I COULDN'T CARE LESS!

Master 'Erbert's Bedroom

ERM... YOU'RE GOING FISHING, AREN'T YOU?

WELL SPOTTED!

GLOWER!

OH, PLEASE CAN I COME WITH YOU?

BEG! PLEAD! GROVEL!

WELL, LET ME THINK...

QUEEK!
... OKAY! MAKE YOURSELF USEFUL AND CARRY MY ROD.
OH, GOODY!
EVER-SO CHUFFED!
WHAT FUN THIS'LL BE!
OINK!
SKIP!
FROLIC!
PRANCE!
R.I.P. A zombie ate poor little Sydney and all we found was a half-chewed kidney
RAAASPP!
COO! WHAT A CREEPY LAKE!
THE FISHING'S GREAT HERE.
ARE YOU GOING TO DIG UP SOME WORMS FOR BAIT?
NO NEED!
BUT YOU DIDN'T BRING ANY BAIT WITH YOU.
YES, I DID!
AND -
AAIIIEEE!
Welcome to ye Black Lagoon!
SLOBBER! DROOL!
SNAP!

DREADLOCK HOLMES

Panel 1:
- WHY ARE YOU STILL HERE?
- WE'RE TRAPPED. IT'S ONLY A FIVER TO GET IN...
- EXIT - £50 TO GET OUT!
- ...BUT IT'S FIFTY QUID TO GET OUT!

Panel 2:
- THE ONLY THINGS THAT WORK ARE THE GAMES IN THE ARCADE, AND THEY AREN'T FREE.
- WELL, WHAT DID THE POLICE SAY WHEN YOU CALLED THEM?

Panel 3:
- UM, I DIDN'T CALL THEM.

Panel 4:
- WELL, A GOOD DETECTIVE NEEDS BACK UP, BEFORE HE SOLVES A MYSTERY!

Panel 5:
- HMM... MARTY RIO? THAT SEEMS FAMILIAR!
- OFFICE OF MARTY RIO
- GOT IT! IT'S AN ANAGRAM OF...

Panel 6:
- ...MORIARTY!
- DREADLOCK HOLMES, WE MEET AGAIN!

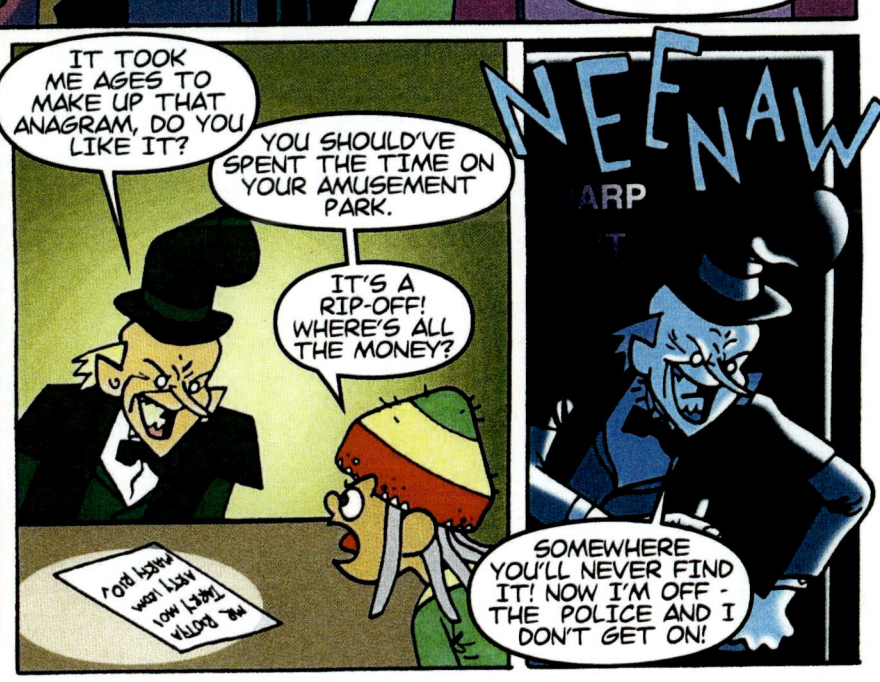

Panel 7:
- IT TOOK ME AGES TO MAKE UP THAT ANAGRAM, DO YOU LIKE IT?
- YOU SHOULD'VE SPENT THE TIME ON YOUR AMUSEMENT PARK. IT'S A RIP-OFF! WHERE'S ALL THE MONEY?

Panel 8:
- NEE NAW
- SOMEWHERE YOU'LL NEVER FIND IT! NOW I'M OFF - THE POLICE AND I DON'T GET ON!

HMM... WHERE WOULD YOU PUT SOMETHING IN AN ARCADE IF YOU WANTED NO-ONE TO BE ABLE TO GET TO IT?
OF COURSE! THE GRABBER MACHINE! NO-ONE EVER GETS ANYTHING OUT OF THOSE!
HMM... THERE ARE LITTLE METAL CLIPS ON THE BAG...
IF I MAGNETISE THE GRABBER...
I SHOULD BE ABLE TO GRAB THE CASH!
COME ON, COME ON - IT'S WORKING!
STREF '06
YIPPEE! GOT IT!
SO -
YOU'LL PAY FOR THIS, DREADLOCK HOLMES!
REFUNDS!
WRONG AGAIN, MORIARTY - WE'RE DUE A REFUND, I THINK!
THAT'S MY BOY!

Advertisement

ONLY £5
FOR YOUR FIRST MONTH*

YOU'LL HAVE A *BLAST* WITH BEANO EVERY WEEK!

WHAT YOU NEED TO KNOW ABOUT A BEANO SUBSCRIPTION:

- **Perfect for kids aged 6 to 12**
- **Price savings on shop price**
- **50 fun-packed issues a year**
- **Free UK delivery included**
- **Sign-up now and cancel any time**
- **Weekly post just for kids**

SAVE 61%

Ask an adult to help.

HOW TO SIGN UP!

VISIT: BEANOSHOP.COM/COMIC

OR

CALL: 0800 318 846

Freephone from UK landlines and mobiles. (Monday-Friday 9am-5pm)

SCAN:

*Direct Debit offer for new customers only. £5 for the first month, then £11 a month. Saving of 61% on the first month based on a newsstand price of £3.25 per issue. Beano is a weekly title publishing 50 issues per year. Prices shown are based on UK delivery and correct at time of going to print. Offers subject to change.

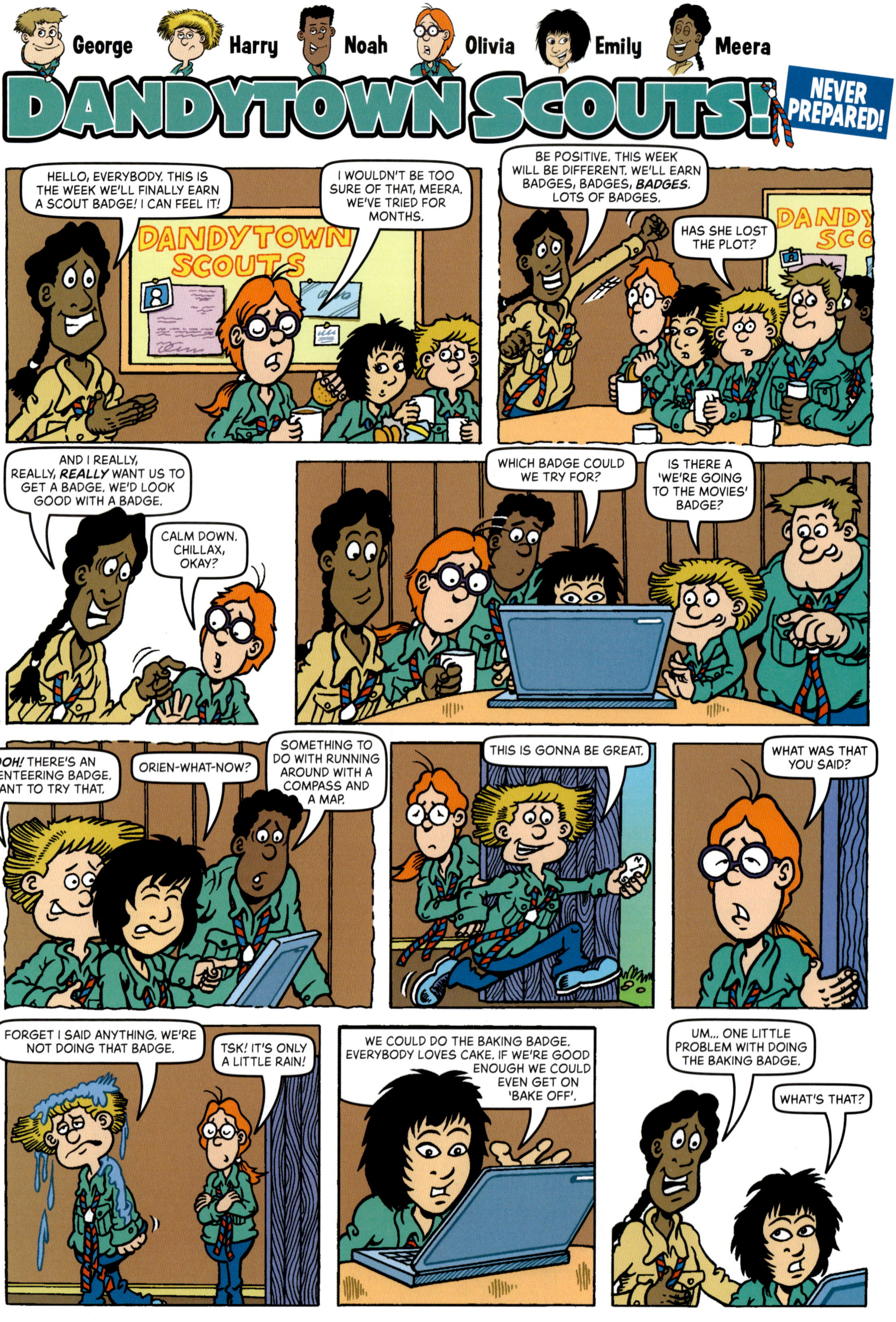
George
Harry
Noah
Olivia
Emily
Meera
DANDYTOWN SCOUTS!
NEVER PREPARED!
HELLO, EVERYBODY. THIS IS THE WEEK WE'LL FINALLY EARN A SCOUT BADGE! I CAN FEEL IT!
DANDYTOWN SCOUTS
I WOULDN'T BE TOO SURE OF THAT, MEERA. WE'VE TRIED FOR MONTHS.
BE POSITIVE. THIS WEEK WILL BE DIFFERENT. WE'LL EARN BADGES, BADGES, BADGES. LOTS OF BADGES.
HAS SHE LOST THE PLOT?
AND I REALLY, REALLY WANT US TO GET A BADGE. WE'D LOOK GOOD WITH A BADGE.
CALM DOWN. CHILLAX, OKAY?
WHICH BADGE COULD WE TRY FOR?
IS THERE A 'WE'RE GOING TO THE MOVIES' BADGE?
OOH! THERE'S AN ORIENTEERING BADGE. I WANT TO TRY THAT.
ORIEN-WHAT-NOW?
SOMETHING TO DO WITH RUNNING AROUND WITH A COMPASS AND A MAP.
THIS IS GONNA BE GREAT.
WHAT WAS THAT YOU SAID?
FORGET I SAID ANYTHING. WE'RE NOT DOING THAT BADGE.
TSK! IT'S ONLY A LITTLE RAIN!
WE COULD DO THE BAKING BADGE. EVERYBODY LOVES CAKE. IF WE'RE GOOD ENOUGH WE COULD EVEN GET ON 'BAKE OFF'.
UM... ONE LITTLE PROBLEM WITH DOING THE BAKING BADGE.
WHAT'S THAT?

CHOMP! CHOMP! CHOMP!
WHAT? WHAT DID WE DO?
YOU ATE THE INGREDIENTS!
RAISINS
IT'S A DISASTER! WE'RE NEVER GOING TO EARN A BADGE.
I KNOW HOW WE CAN EARN A BADGE... SORT OF.
WHAT'S THE PLAN?
ARE WE HAVING A PLAN? WE USUALLY JUST HOPE FOR THE BEST.
SO...
DON'T BE SAD, DAISY. IT'LL BE ALL RIGHT.
DAISY? WHAT'S HE TALKING ABOUT? WHO'S DAISY? I'M MEERA.
WHATEVER YOU SAY, JESSICA.
RAISINS
JESSI-WHAT? WHY DID YOU CALL ME JESSICA?
MY NAME'S MEERA, REMEMBER?
HEAR THAT, DAVE?
TOTALLY DID, AGNES.
THIS IS TERRIBLE. WE NEED TO BE REMINDED OF EVERYBODY'S REAL NAMES.
IF YOU SAY SO, KYLIE.
WE GOT BADGES AFTER ALL.
A NAME BADGE, BUT STILL A BADGE.
YAY! GO US!
THAT'S NOT WHAT I... OH, FORGET IT. THEY'RE A START, I SUPPOSE.
NOAH
OLIVIA
EMILY
HARRY
GEORGE

DESPERATE DAN
CONGRATULATIONS, DANNY! YOU ARE NOW THE NEW WORLD CHAMPION!
WELL DONE, DANNY!
GOOD FOR YOU, DANNY! YOU'VE EVEN BEATEN UNCLE DAN!
How it happened—
THIS IS THE WORLD HIGH DIVING CHAMP, DAN. IN HIS WINNING DIVE HE DID FOUR SOMERSAULTS BEFORE REACHING THE WATER.
ONLY FOUR? IS THAT ALL HE COULD MANAGE?
WORLD HIGH DIVE CHAMP
WE'D BETTER KEEP BACK, SHERIFF. UNCLE DAN WILL HIT THE WATER WITH SUCH A SPLASH, HE MIGHT WASH US OFF THE PIER!
I'LL SHOW HIM!
PIER
COME ON, MISTER. WE'LL WATCH FROM THE BEACH!
A COUPLE OF LITTLE JUMPS FIRST.
DOWN AND—
WHUMP
CREAK
GROAN
HUP! AND—
WHAT THE BLAZES?
HELP!
DOWN— AND THEN SPRING!
THUD
I'M HIGH ENOUGH TO DO ABOUT A DOZEN SOMERSAULTS!
HELP!
AMAZING! ELEVEN SOMERSAULTS BY DAN!
SPLOSH
AND THERE'S THE SHERIFF—HE'S DONE THIRTEEN!
LOOK AT YOUNG DANNY. HE'S DONE SEVENTEEN!
DANNY WINS!
HO-HO-HO! GUESS I DON'T MIND ONLY COMING THIRD. THEY SAY I CAUSED THE BIGGEST SPLASH—BUT THE SHERIFF CAUSED THE DIRTIEST ONE! HERE HE COMES!
NEVER MIND, SHERIFF! YOU WIN SECOND PRIZE!
DOHHH!
HO-HO! HE CAME DOWN IN A PIG STY!

BERYL the PERIL
RATS!
GETAWAY!
I'LL BE SAFE UNDER HERE.
CAN'T STAY HERE FOREVER, THOUGH.
So —
Soon —
THAT'S ME HOME SAFE — IT'S GONE.
WHAT'S GONE?
Reader's voice
THAT BLACK CLOUD. IT WAS FOLLOWIN' ME AN' I JUST HATE GETTIN' CAUGHT IN THE PESKY RAIN!

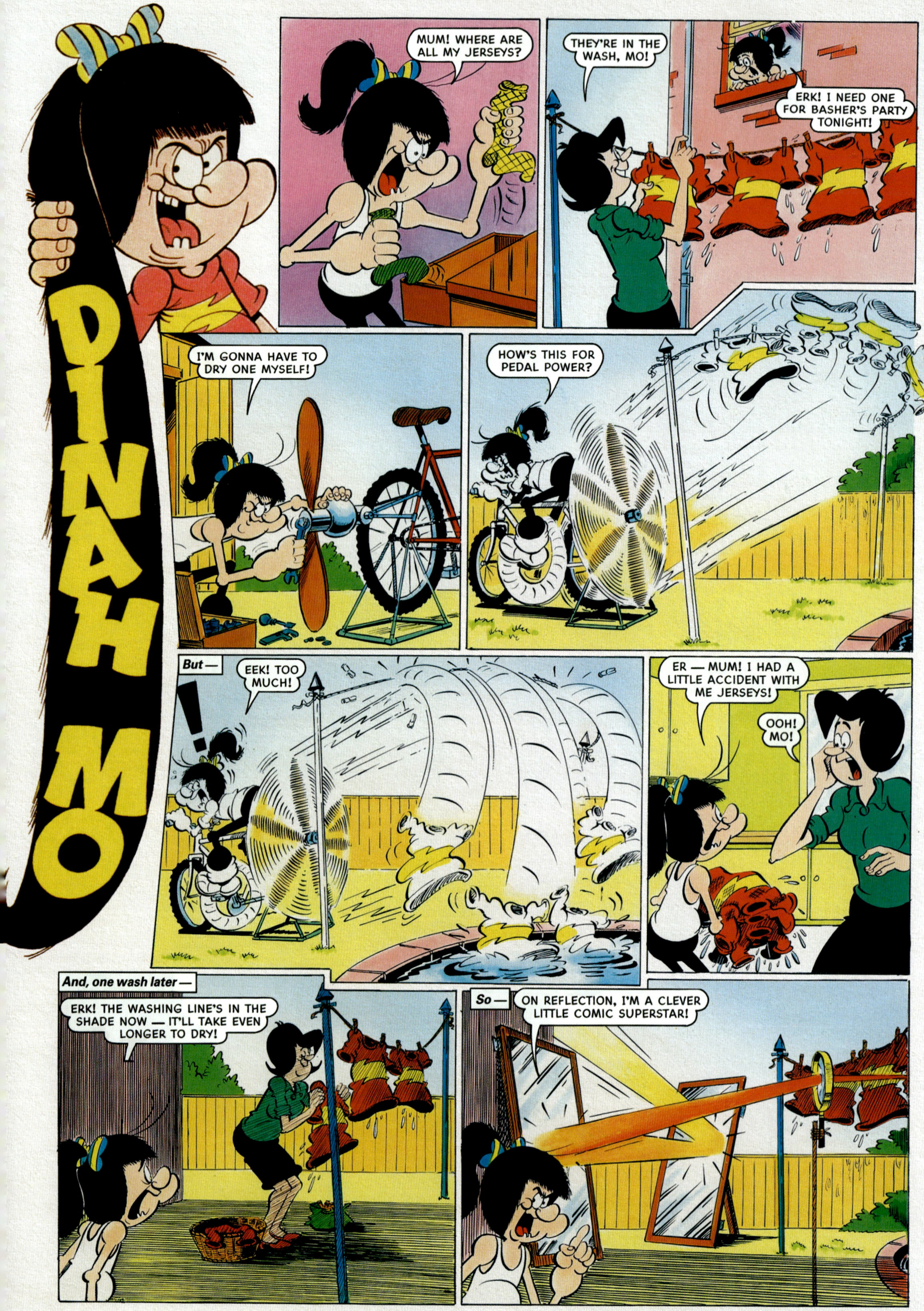
DINAH MO
MUM! WHERE ARE ALL MY JERSEYS?
THEY'RE IN THE WASH, MO!
ERK! I NEED ONE FOR BASHER'S PARTY TONIGHT!
I'M GONNA HAVE TO DRY ONE MYSELF!
HOW'S THIS FOR PEDAL POWER?
But —
EEK! TOO MUCH!
!
ER — MUM! I HAD A LITTLE ACCIDENT WITH ME JERSEYS!
OOH! MO!
And, one wash later —
ERK! THE WASHING LINE'S IN THE SHADE NOW — IT'LL TAKE EVEN LONGER TO DRY!
So —
ON REFLECTION, I'M A CLEVER LITTLE COMIC SUPERSTAR!

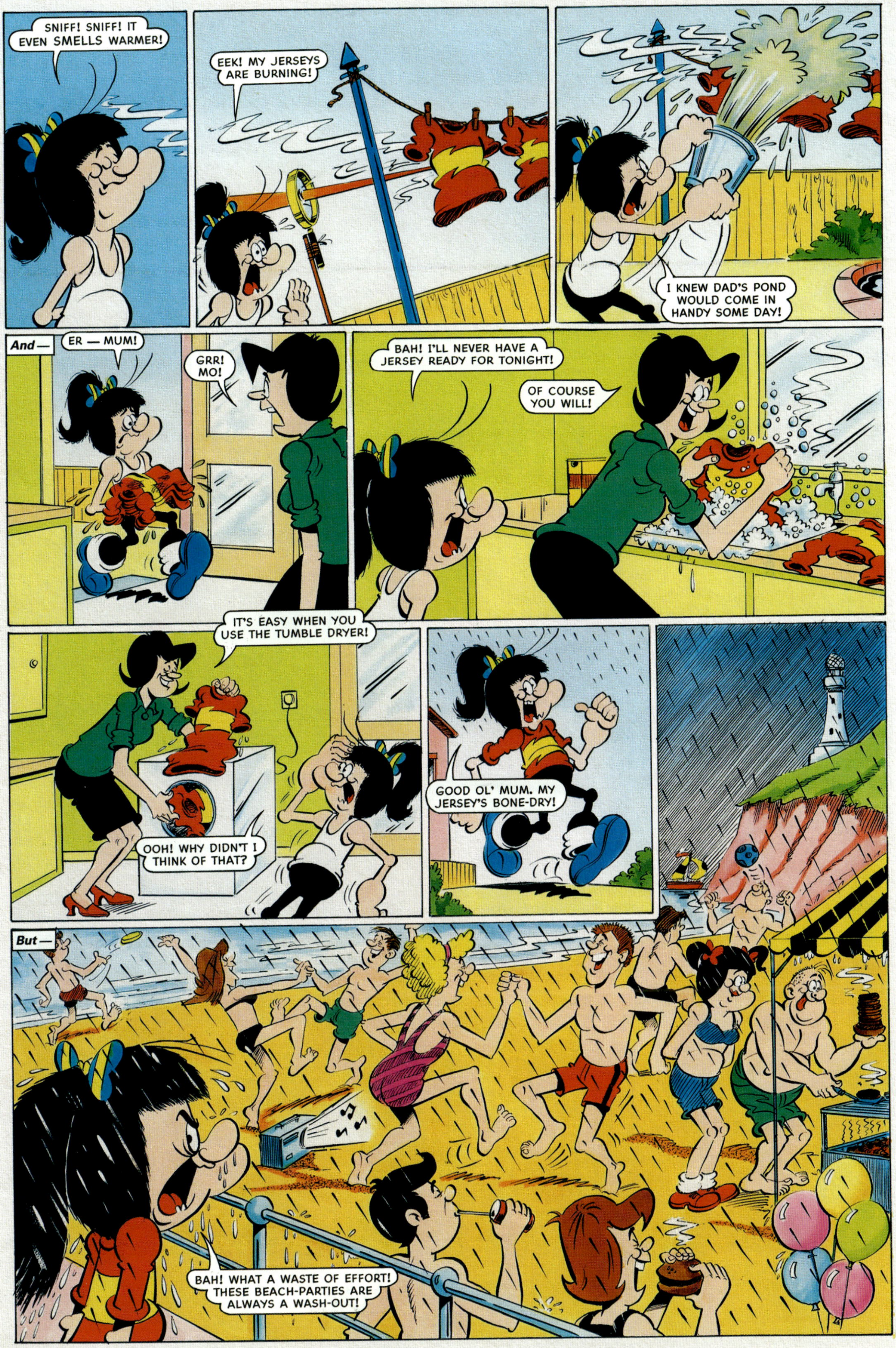
SNIFF! SNIFF! IT EVEN SMELLS WARMER!
EEK! MY JERSEYS ARE BURNING!
I KNEW DAD'S POND WOULD COME IN HANDY SOME DAY!
And—
ER — MUM!
GRR! MO!
BAH! I'LL NEVER HAVE A JERSEY READY FOR TONIGHT!
OF COURSE YOU WILL!
IT'S EASY WHEN YOU USE THE TUMBLE DRYER!
OOH! WHY DIDN'T I THINK OF THAT?
GOOD OL' MUM. MY JERSEY'S BONE-DRY!
But—
BAH! WHAT A WASTE OF EFFORT! THESE BEACH-PARTIES ARE ALWAYS A WASH-OUT!

CORPORAL CLOTT
Ok, Clott, I need you to give this new all-terrain vehicle a test drive. Try it on the off road track.
Will do Mr Grumbly, Your Majesty, Sir!
I've got some biscuits that need eating.
Er, Sir...
Capering Captains, Clott!!! I didn't even hear you start it!!!
Yeah. I don't really understand how I did it.
The use of one crane later...
You can't be trusted on your own, Clott. You great lumbering fathead! I'll have to come with you.
Start her up.
Arrrgh!
Forwards! Not backwards!
CRASH!
Grumbly and Clott spend the day testing the new vehicle...
Well, it's surprisingly good on hills...
Now get us down from here!!!
Well, it deals with water well.
But I'm not wearing my trunks!!! So back up!
Nigel Auchterlounie
Just take me back to my quarters, Clott. I've had enough.
So...
Here we are, Sir. Home again!
Where? I can't see my quarters.
Arrrrgh! Clott, you idiot!!!

WE'S GOT THE BIGGEST WATER-BLASTER!
AN' WE'S GONNA USE IT!!
CUDDLES AND DIMPLES
JUST WHEN YOU THOUGHT IT WAS SAFE... TO GO BACK TO THE BEACH!!!
Mmm...
SWOOSH!
...mmff!?!
COO, WHAT A DREAM-BOAT.
AIN'T I JUST?
SPLOOSH!
WHAT A BALDY, MORE LIKE!
AIN'T HE JUST?
LET 'EM 'AVE IT, BRUV.
'IS IS FUN!
HEY, WHAT'S...
SLOOSH!
...THAT?
US!
?
TAP!
WHAT'S THE BIG IDEA? YOU WISE GUYS HAVE DRAINED THE WHOLE SEA!
C'MERE!
YIKES! WE'S OUTTA HERE!!!

HYDE & SHRIEK
DANDY
MR. SHRIEK IS TAKING ME TO THE ZOO - THAT SHOULD BE FUN!
ZOO
FROLIC!
SKIP!
PRANCE!
LET'S GO AND LOOK AT THE MAN-EATING LIONS!
NO WAY!
BOWEL-LOOSENING
ROAAAR!
HOW ABOUT THE MAN-EATING SHARKS, THEN?
AGAIN - NO WAY!
AQUARIU
SPLASH! GNASH! CHOMP!
IS THERE ANYTHING HERE THAT ISN'T MAN-EATING?
WILLIES!
NOT SURE - THE GIBBONS, PERHAPS?
AHA! THAT LOOKS MORE MY SPEED. THERE'LL BE LOTS OF FLUFFY BUNNIES AND GOATS AND THINGS IN HERE!
BALEFUL GLARE!
PETTING ZOO
SIMPER! TWITTER! GUSH!
BUT -
HUH! THERE'S NOTHING HERE BUT SLEEPING BATS!
DEEPLY MIFFED!
I'D KEEP MY VOICE DOWN IF I WERE YOU!
AND -
TOO LATE - YOU'VE WOKEN UP THE VAMPIRE BATS!
FLAP!
FLUTTER!
DROOL!
AAAIIIEEEE!
FLAP! GUZZLE! GORGE! SLURP! SQUEEK!
PEOPLE LIKE YOU DRIVE ME MAD - CAN'T YOU READ THE SIGNS?
BELCH!
DO NOT FEED THE ANIMALS!

Advertisement

JOIN DENNIS & FRIENDS ON BLAM ADVENTURES!

TOLD WITH FUNNY PICTURES

BOOK + COMIC = BOOMIC!

BEANO — AVAILABLE WHEREVER BOOKS ARE SOLD — BEANO.COM

DREADLOCK HOLMES

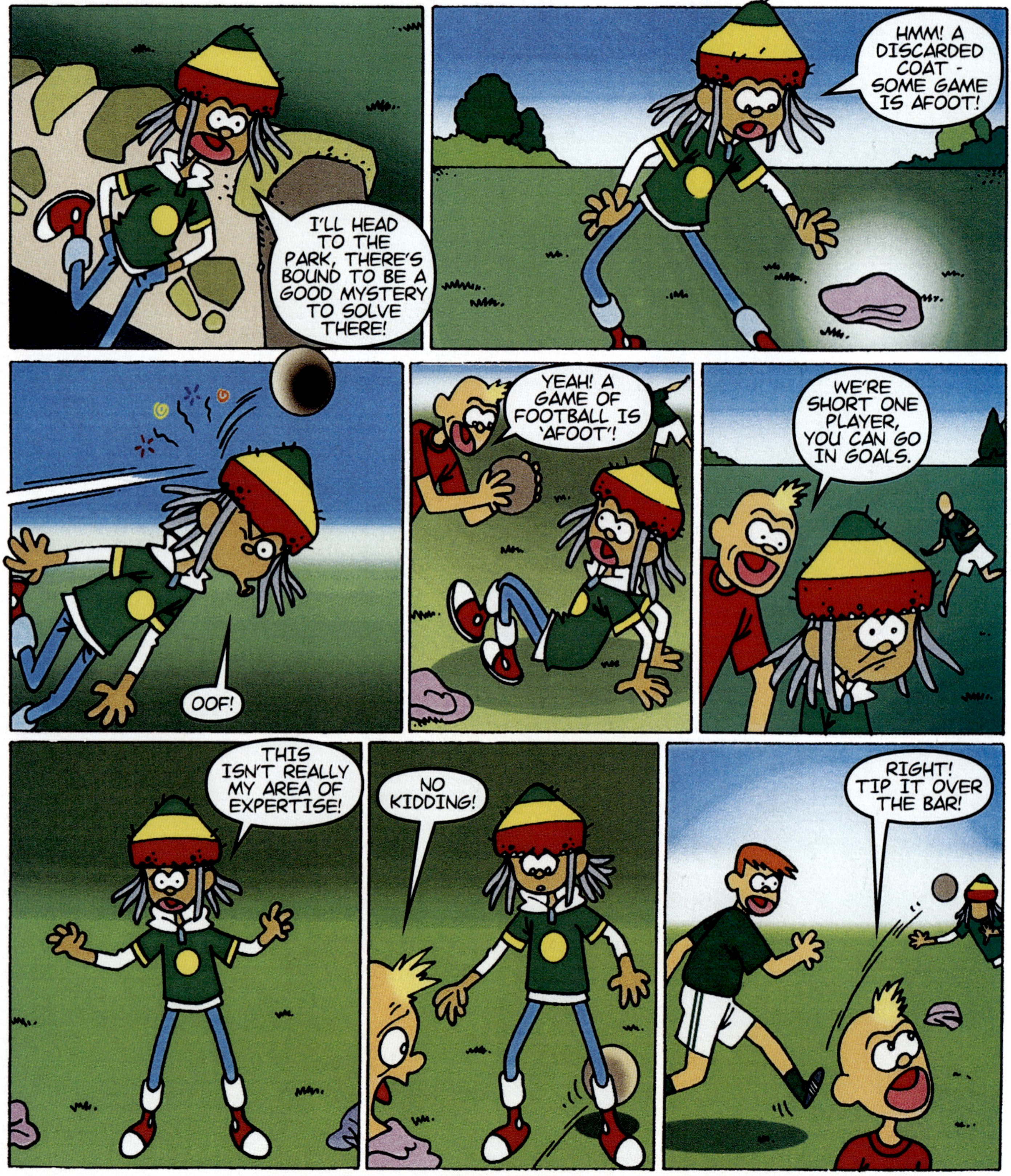

ER... WHAT BAR?
USELESS!
BUT THERE IS NO BAR!
EVERY BOY KNOWS THE EXACT HEIGHT OF AN IMAGINARY CROSSBAR!
TRY PLAYING UP FRONT, YOU'LL DO LESS DAMAGE!
I HOPE I'M ABLE TO KICK THE BALL STRAIGHT!
OFFSIDE!
EH?
WHAT DOES 'OFFSIDE' MEAN?
YOU HAVE TO BE AT LEAST IN LINE WITH THE LAST DEFENDER WHEN THE BALL IS INITIALLY KICKED...
THAT'S IT - I'M OFF! FOOTBALL IS MORE OF A MYSTERY TO ME THAN THE MARY CELESTE, THE LOCH NESS MONSTER AND THE BERMUDA TRIANGLE PUT TOGETHER!

MY MUM'S A ...
SUPER VILLAIN
SWEETIE VILLE
KANE VILLE
LAYLA VILLE
HYDRA
CERBERUS
TIM
UH-OH! MY PARENTS ARE WHISPERING.
THAT CAN ONLY MEAN THEY'RE HATCHING A PLAN TO TAKE OVER THE WORLD!
SO, IT'S SETTLED?
TODAY WE TAKE OVER... THE BIT OF STREET JUST OUTSIDE OUR HOUSE!
THE BIT OF STREET JUST OUTSIDE OUR HOUSE?
YES!
PARKING IS A NIGHTMARE!
LAST NIGHT YOUR DAD HAD TO PARK DOWN NEAR THE FISH SHOP!
NO MORE, THANKS TO MY ARMY OF CONES!
ARMY? THERE ARE ONLY TWO!
DRIVE ON, DEREK! I'VE GOT CONES OUT!
THIS IS A PUBLIC STREET, YOU CAN'T DO THAT!
DIDN'T YOU HEAR ME? I SAID, I'VE GOT CONES OUT!
AND I'M GONNA PARK ON THEM!
GET HIM!
ARRGH! ATTACK OF THE CONES!
THEY WORK PERFECTLY! I'LL GET THE CAR.
I USUALLY TRY TO STOP MY PARENTS' PLANS, BUT THIS IS JUST ABOUT PARKING OUTSIDE THE HOUSE.
BUT...
SORRY, YOU CANNOT PARK HERE!
WHAT? BUT YOU'RE MY CONES!
GET HIM!
ARRGH!
I CREATED YOU! HAVE SOME RESPECT!
THIS STREET IS OURS, OLD MAN!
THERE WAS ONLY SUPPOSED TO BE TWO OF YOU! THIS IS WORRYING!
POP!

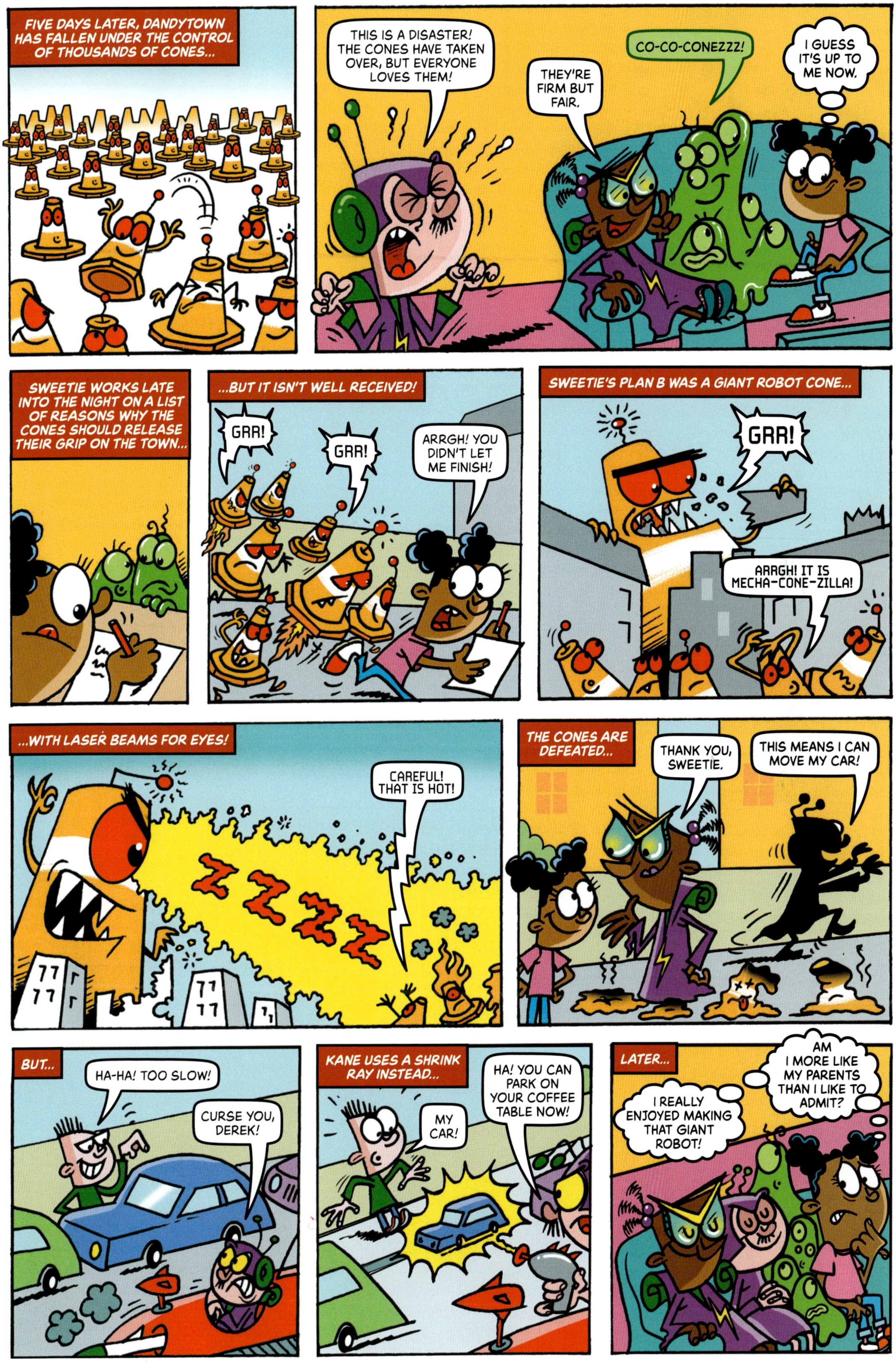
FIVE DAYS LATER, DANDYTOWN HAS FALLEN UNDER THE CONTROL OF THOUSANDS OF CONES...
THIS IS A DISASTER! THE CONES HAVE TAKEN OVER, BUT EVERYONE LOVES THEM!
THEY'RE FIRM BUT FAIR.
CO-CO-CONEZZZ!
I GUESS IT'S UP TO ME NOW.
SWEETIE WORKS LATE INTO THE NIGHT ON A LIST OF REASONS WHY THE CONES SHOULD RELEASE THEIR GRIP ON THE TOWN...
...BUT IT ISN'T WELL RECEIVED!
GRR!
GRR!
ARRGH! YOU DIDN'T LET ME FINISH!
SWEETIE'S PLAN B WAS A GIANT ROBOT CONE...
GRR!
ARRGH! IT IS MECHA-CONE-ZILLA!
...WITH LASER BEAMS FOR EYES!
CAREFUL! THAT IS HOT!
ZZZZ
THE CONES ARE DEFEATED...
THANK YOU, SWEETIE.
THIS MEANS I CAN MOVE MY CAR!
BUT...
HA-HA! TOO SLOW!
CURSE YOU, DEREK!
KANE USES A SHRINK RAY INSTEAD...
MY CAR!
HA! YOU CAN PARK ON YOUR COFFEE TABLE NOW!
LATER...
I REALLY ENJOYED MAKING THAT GIANT ROBOT!
AM I MORE LIKE MY PARENTS THAN I LIKE TO ADMIT?

Desperate DAN'S

Holiday Snaps

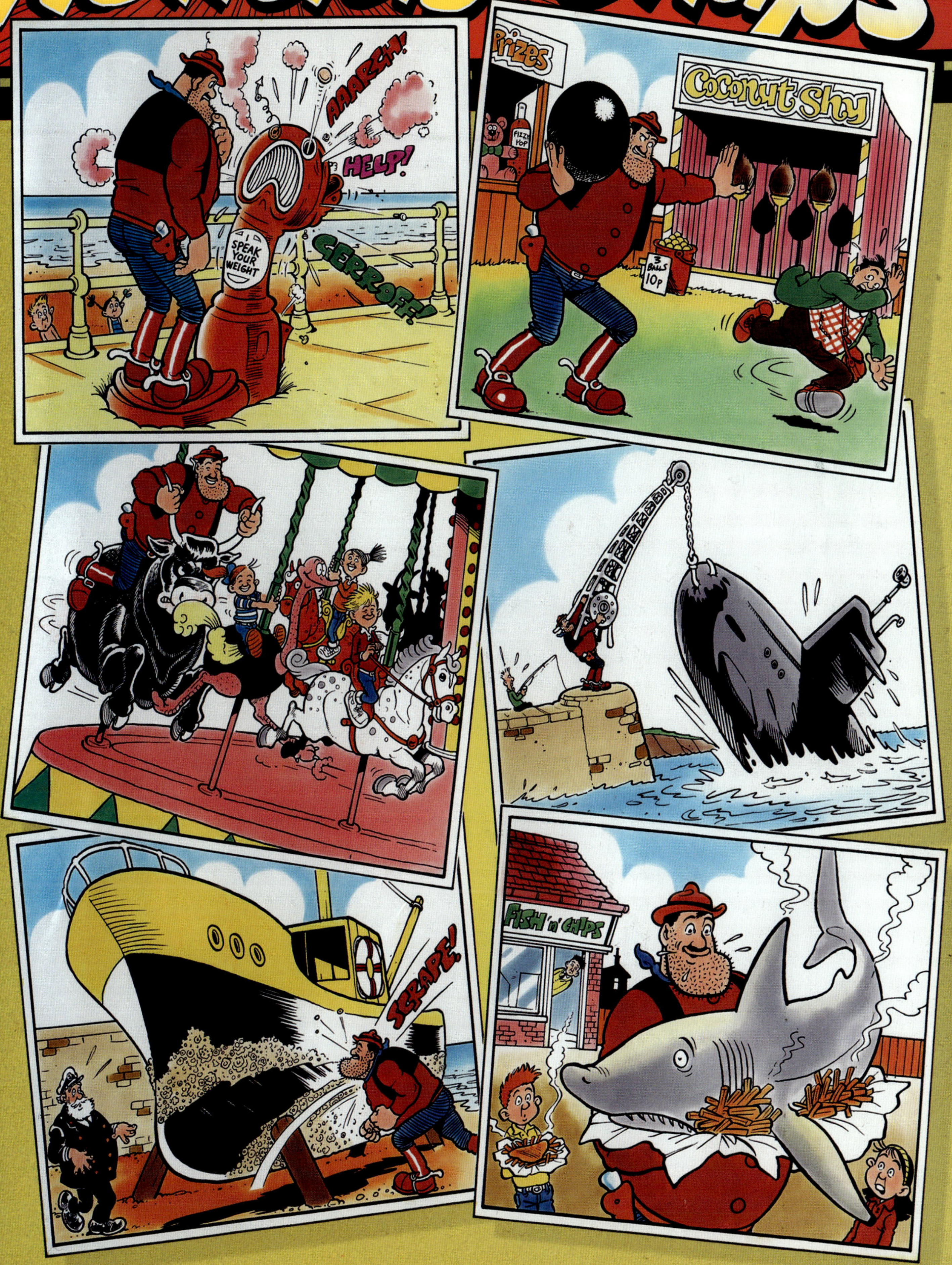

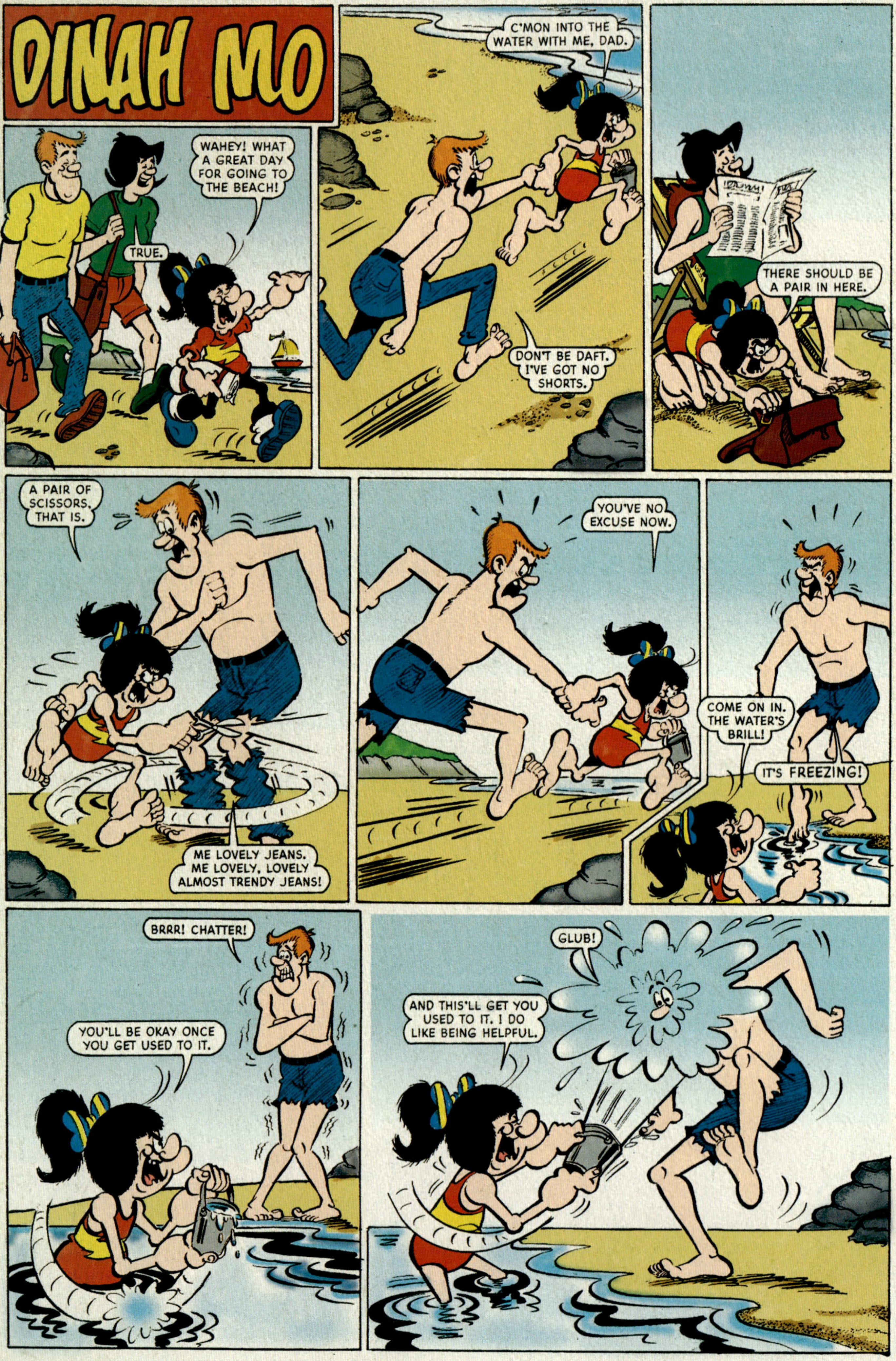
DINAH MO
WAHEY! WHAT A GREAT DAY FOR GOING TO THE BEACH!
TRUE.
C'MON INTO THE WATER WITH ME, DAD.
DON'T BE DAFT. I'VE GOT NO SHORTS.
THERE SHOULD BE A PAIR IN HERE.
A PAIR OF SCISSORS, THAT IS.
ME LOVELY JEANS. ME LOVELY, LOVELY ALMOST TRENDY JEANS!
YOU'VE NO EXCUSE NOW.
COME ON IN. THE WATER'S BRILL!
IT'S FREEZING!
BRRR! CHATTER!
YOU'LL BE OKAY ONCE YOU GET USED TO IT.
GLUB!
AND THIS'LL GET YOU USED TO IT. I DO LIKE BEING HELPFUL.

AAAGH! I'LL MARMALISE YOU!
GOOD OL' DAD. HE'S COMING IN, NOW.
OUT OF THE WATER, YOU. IF I'M GOING SWIMMING, I DON'T WANT YOU NEAR ME. I DON'T TRUST YOU.
BOO! WHAT A BIG BABY.
I'LL JUST HAVE TO DO A SPOT OF FISHING THEN.
YA-HOO! BOMBS AWAY!
GOTTEM!
SQUEAL!
YOUR FATHER MUST BE REALLY ENJOYING HIMSELF. HE'S BEEN IN THE WATER A LONG TIME.
HE HAS, HASN'T HE?
I WONDER IF THAT'S GOT ANYTHING TO DO WITH MY CATCH?
THROW 'EM BACK, GIRL! I'LL BE ARRESTED!
FLY FISHING, MO?

BERYL THE PERIL
WHAT A PERFECT DAY FOR . . .
. . . SLAPPING ON THE SUNTAN LOTION AN' LAZING ABOUT.
OOO, YOU'LL BE SORRY — SUNBATHING CAN BE BAD FOR YOU.
WRAP UP! I'M PROTECTED!
SPLAT!
BLARRT!
ROTTER!
OF COURSE, THIS MEANS WAR!
CHARGE!
CLATTER!
GOTTIM!
ANYONE FOR . . .
THIS COULD BE GOOD.
GRAAGH!
. . . A MONSTER!

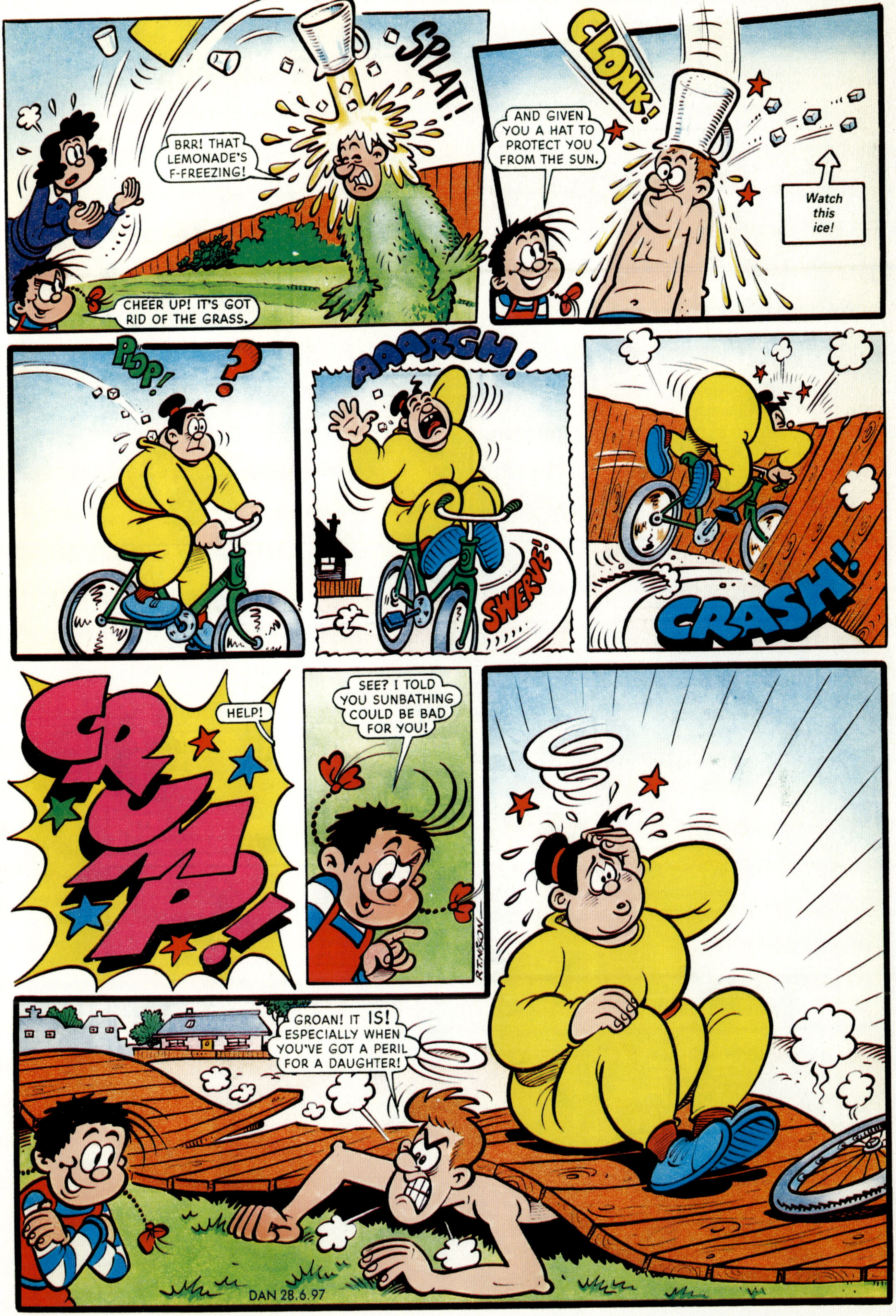
SPLAT!
BRR! THAT LEMONADE'S F-FREEZING!
CHEER UP! IT'S GOT RID OF THE GRASS.
CLONK!
AND GIVEN YOU A HAT TO PROTECT YOU FROM THE SUN.
Watch this ice!
PLOP!
AAARGH!
SWERVE!
CRASH!
CRUNCH!
HELP!
SEE? I TOLD YOU SUNBATHING COULD BE BAD FOR YOU!
GROAN! IT IS! ESPECIALLY WHEN YOU'VE GOT A PERIL FOR A DAUGHTER!
DAN 28.6.97

CORPORAL CLOTT

Panel 1: In this training exercise you're going to learn how to build a temporary bridge called a pontoon bridge. — Cool!

Panel 2: It's simple really. All you need is a few decks and some pontoons which float on the water. The decks go from one side of the river across the tops of the pontoons to the other side.

Panel 3: It's hard to imagine how you might get it wrong...

Panel 4: AND YET YOU HAVE!!! Don't build the middle bit first!!! Now we're floating down river!!!

Nigel Auchterlounie

Panel 5: Oh yeah! Without connecting it to the riverbank there's nothing to stop us from going off the top of that waterfall. — Yes, that's ri... that what!?!

Panel 6: AAARGH!

Panel 7: What happened to Mr Grumbly?

Panel 8: ARRRRGH! A shark!!! — Clott!!! *BURST!*

Panel 9: Here's a cup of hot cocoa, Sir. Still no sign of Corporal Clott, Sir. — I'm sure he'll turn up soon.

Panel 10: Nice of Colonel Grumbly to tie me to this pontoon to stop me falling off.

Advertisement

GET YOUR HANDS ON OUR BLAMTASTIC ANNUAL!

FEATURING YOUR FAVOURITE CHARACTERS: DENNIS, GNASHER, MINNIE, JJ, DANGEROUS DAN AND MORE!

OUT NOW FOR £11.99! RRP

LOOK OUT FOR THE 2025 ANNUAL COMING IN AUGUST!

BEANO Available at all major retailers

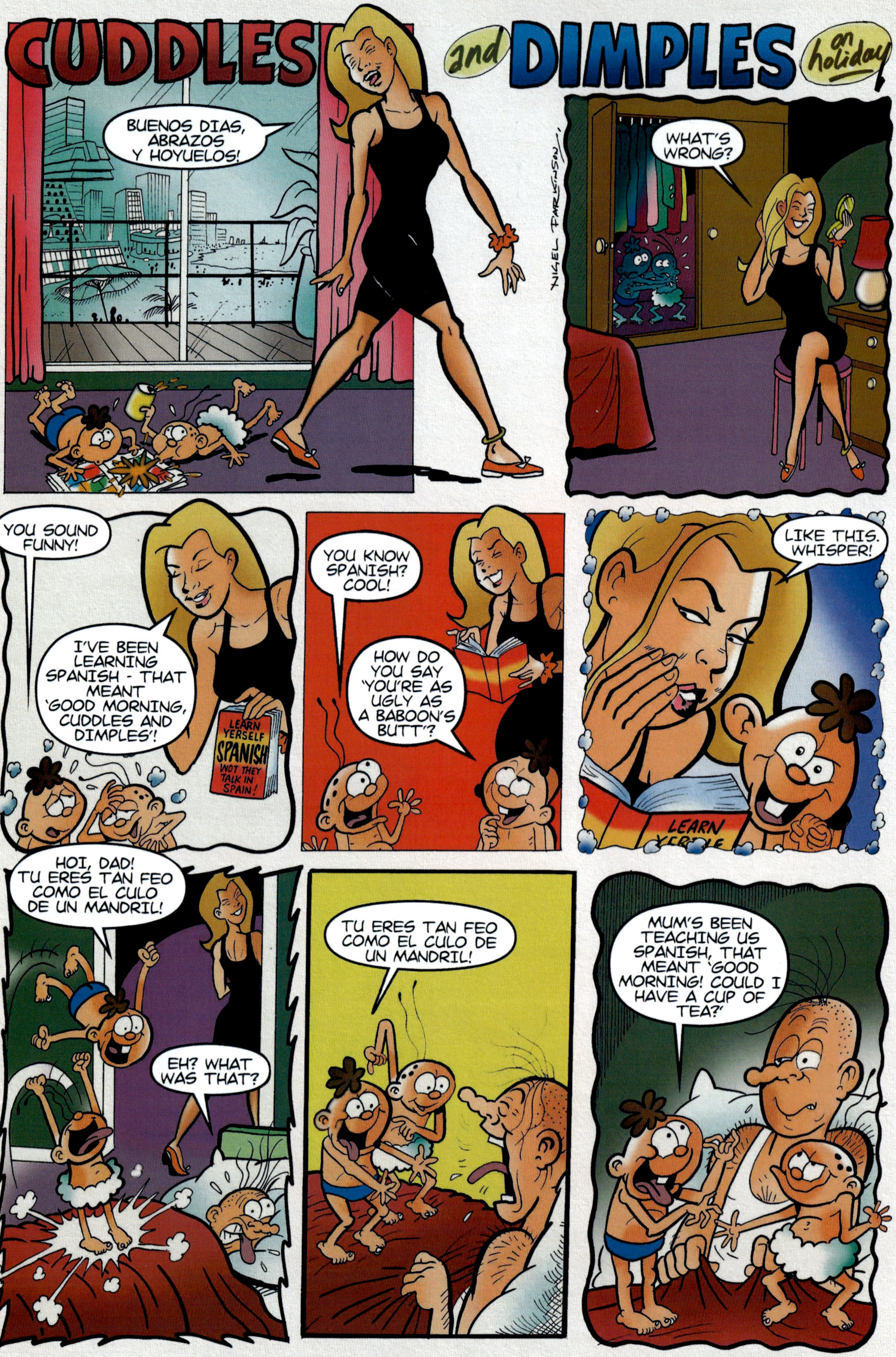
CUDDLES and DIMPLES on holiday
BUENOS DIAS, ABRAZOS Y HOYUELOS!
NIGEL PARKINSON
WHAT'S WRONG?
YOU SOUND FUNNY!
I'VE BEEN LEARNING SPANISH - THAT MEANT 'GOOD MORNING, CUDDLES AND DIMPLES'!
LEARN YERSELF SPANISH WOT THEY TALK IN SPAIN!
YOU KNOW SPANISH? COOL!
HOW DO YOU SAY 'YOU'RE AS UGLY AS A BABOON'S BUTT'?
LIKE THIS. WHISPER!
LEARN
HOI, DAD! TU ERES TAN FEO COMO EL CULO DE UN MANDRIL!
EH? WHAT WAS THAT?
TU ERES TAN FEO COMO EL CULO DE UN MANDRIL!
MUM'S BEEN TEACHING US SPANISH, THAT MEANT 'GOOD MORNING! COULD I HAVE A CUP OF TEA?'

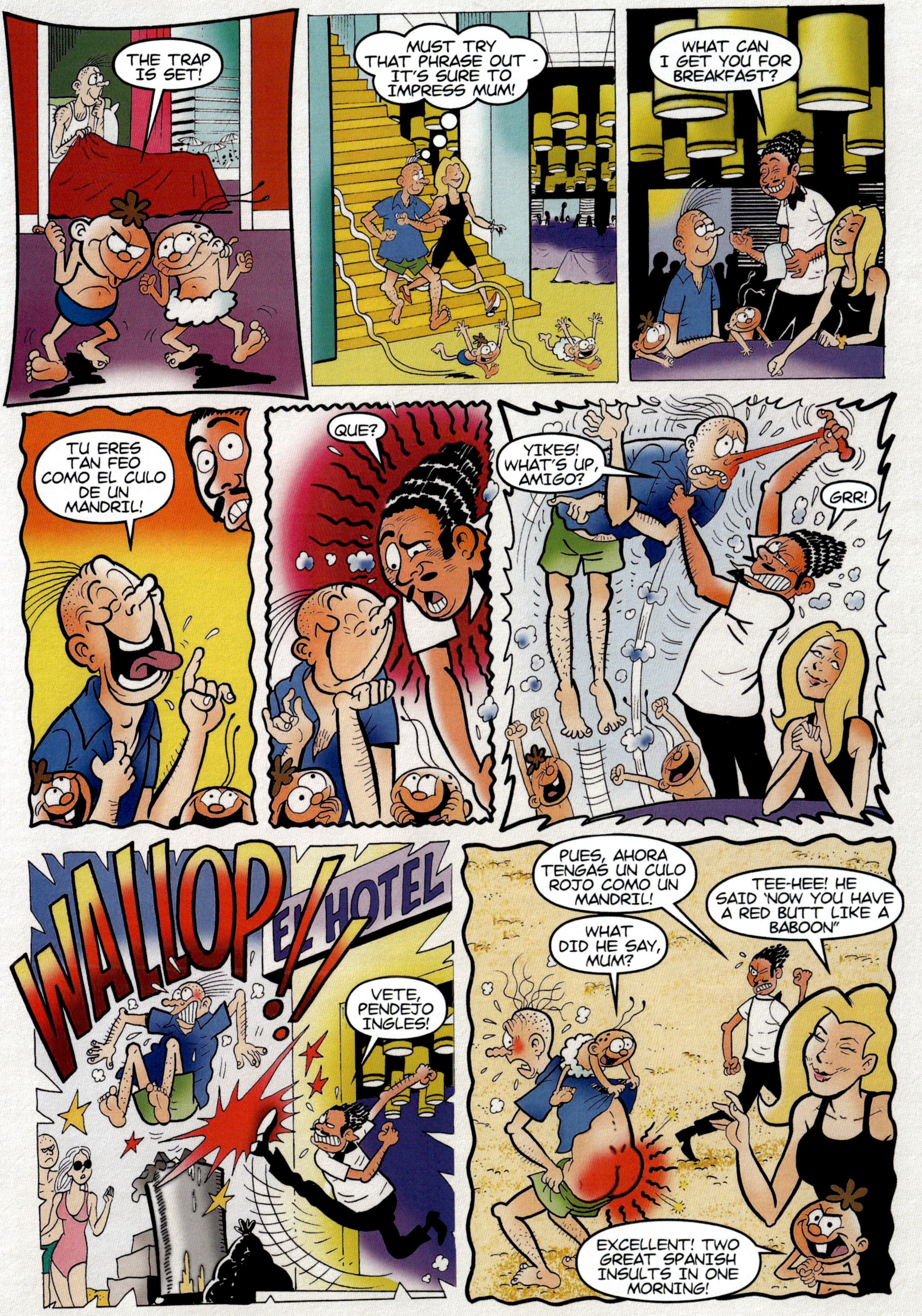
THE TRAP IS SET!
MUST TRY THAT PHRASE OUT - IT'S SURE TO IMPRESS MUM!
WHAT CAN I GET YOU FOR BREAKFAST?
TU ERES TAN FEO COMO EL CULO DE UN MANDRIL!
QUE?
YIKES! WHAT'S UP, AMIGO?
GRR!
WALLOP!
EL HOTEL
VETE, PENDEJO INGLES!
PUES, AHORA TENGAS UN CULO ROJO COMO UN MANDRIL!
WHAT DID HE SAY, MUM?
TEE-HEE! HE SAID 'NOW YOU HAVE A RED BUTT LIKE A BABOON"
EXCELLENT! TWO GREAT SPANISH INSULTS IN ONE MORNING!

HYDE & SHRIEK
DANDY
II
HUMPH! I'M FED UP BEING STUCK IN THIS STUFFY, OLD CASTLE EVERY DAY.
I'M GOING OUT FOR SOME FRESH AIR.
GASP! 'FRESH' AIR? DID YOU SAY 'FRESH' AIR?
WHAT WOULD ANYONE WANT WITH NASTY, HORRIBLE FRESH AIR ...
STOMP!
.... WHEN YOU CAN ENJOY THE SPLENDID, NOXIOUS NIFF OF THE FRACTURED MEDIEVAL DRAINS?
POO-OOO!
PUNGENT PLOPPY PONG!
THEN -
GO ON, SNIFF UP THOSE FUMES!
SHOVE!
BLEEURGH!
AAGH! THE FESTERING STENCH OF DECAY!
STUPEFYING STINK!
COLLAPSE!
CROMBIE THE ZOMBIE'S GIVING HIS ARMPITS THEIR ANNUAL SUMMER AIRING. SNIFF!
MOANNNN! GROANNN!
EVIL UNDEAD STENCH!
HOOTER RECOILING WITH HORROR!
EAGER SNIFF!
PUTRID POOOO!
RANK ROTTEN REEK!
EXTREME CLOSE-UP OF STEAMING ZOMBIE ARMPIT FOR SERIOUS WEIRDOES!

AND -
GET A WHIFF OF THAT ...
TWITCH!
SNIFF!
INHALE!
... MY ANCIENT UNDERPANT COLLECTION IS MOULDERING NICELY IN THIS HEATWAVE!
PHWAAW!
SWEATY HUMMM!
SICK BUCKET
GREAT GRANDAD'S THERMALS
AND GUESS WHAT I HAD FOR LUNCH TODAY?
ER ... WHAT?
EVIL LEER!
DIABOLICAL STRAININGS!
RADISH, KIPPER AND BOILED EGG VINDALOO!
AIIEEE!
'ERBERT'S PANTS
CATACLYSMIC THUNDEROUS PHWOMPPP!
PAAARPLE!
BLAAART!
PHOOORT!
I CAN'T TAKE ANY MORE GHASTLY GUFFS.
HALF-GASSED GIBBERINGS!
I'VE GOT TO GET OUTSIDE!
I NEED TO FEEL THE WIND IN MY HAIR ...
666
... THE SUN ON MY ZITS ...
... AND THE ... GLEEUMPH!
COMPOST IN YOUR NOSTRILS?
SKID!
SMELLY SPLEURGE!
Mr. Shriek's Steaming Compost Heap. Est. 1572
HUMM! STEAM!
I DON'T CARE! I'M OUTSIDE! I'M FREE! I'M IN THE FRESH ....
ROMP!
FROLIC!
CAREFREE ROMPINGS!

AWFUL EGGY HUMMM OF MALIGNANT MARSH GAS!
UTTERLY AWESOME STINK!
Ye Swamp of Nostril-Numbing Niffs.
.... AIR?
?!
CHOKE! GAG! HEAVE!
Ye Ancient Reeking Stench-pits.
Beware of the nasty guff!
BLURPLE! BLOYP!
Ye Stinking Stagnant Duckpond.
Beware of very rude parping ducks.
OOZE!
STEAM!
BALOYP!
SPLOOOO!
THRRRAART!
PONG!
EVIL QUONK!
POOT!
SNIFF!
PHWAAARRT!
Mr. Shriek's Festering Fungus Patch.
QUACKLE!
JET-PROPELLED PWAAARRRRPPP!
YEEUCH! IT'S EVEN STINKIER OUT THERE THAN IT IS IN HERE!
FLEE!
AAH! THE GOOD OLD CASTLE DRAINS!
I'VE SAID IT BEFORE AND I'LL SAY IT AGAIN ... THAT LAD IS WEIRD!
DEEP SNIFF!
PUTRID STENCH!
-TOM PATERSON-

WANT MORE
BEANO
FUN?
AWESOME PRIZES!
HILARIOUS JOKES!
THE COOLEST COMICS!
OUTRAGEOUS PRANKS!
EPIC PUZZLES!
THEN GET BEANO
EVERY WEDNESDAY!

DREADLOCK HOLMES

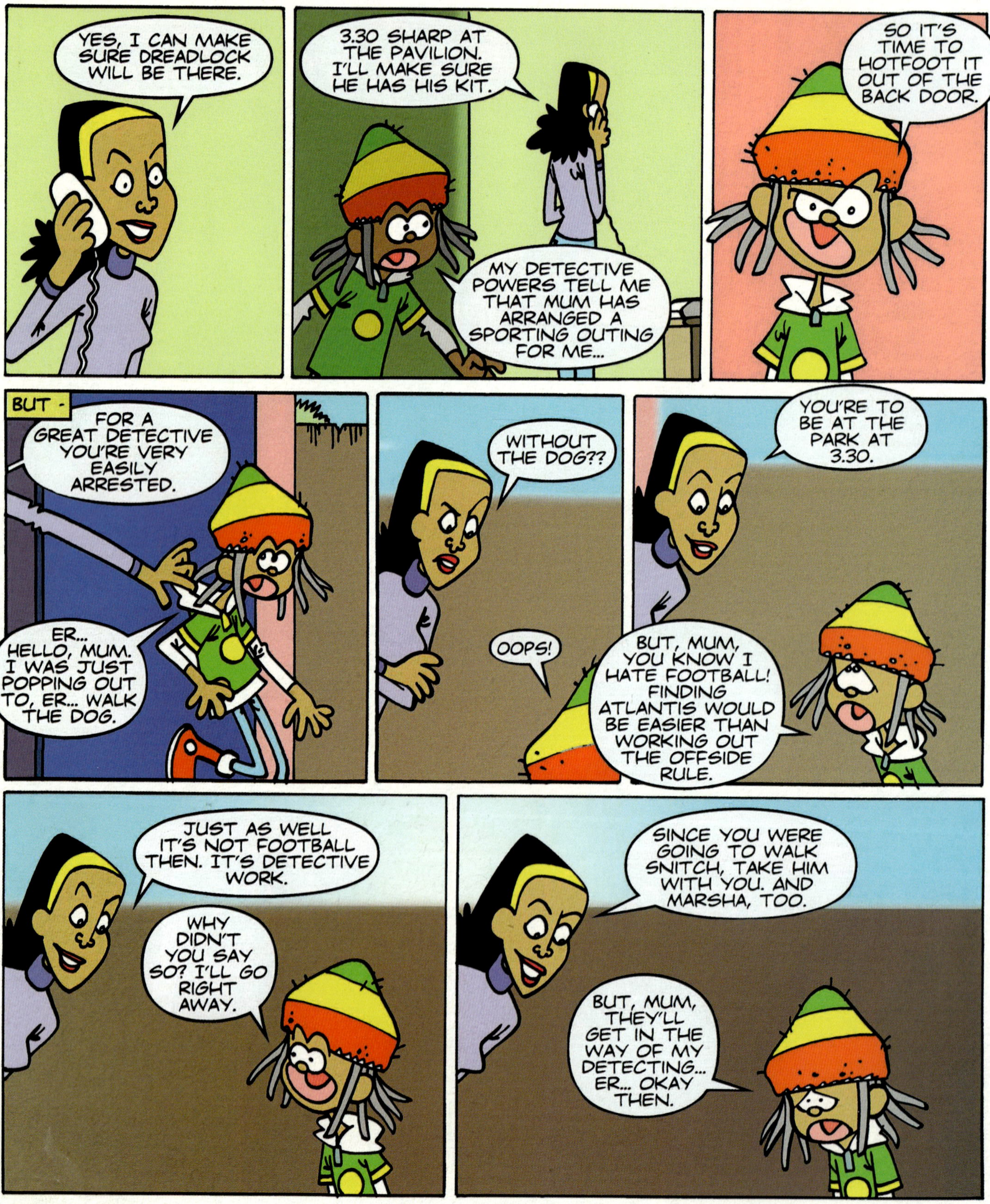

THEY MUST NEED ME TO FIND SOMETHING IMPORTANT TO CALL ME IN SPECIALLY.
IT CAN'T BE IMPORTANT OR THEY'D HAVE ASKED FOR A REAL DETECTIVE.
JUST BECAUSE I'M A BOY DOESN'T MEAN I'M NOT A REAL DETECTIVE!
YOU TWO ARE NOT TO GET UNDER MY FEET WHEN I'M WORKING.
GRRR!
GRRR!
CHOCOLATE HUNT
IT'LL BE DIFFICULT TO FIND ANYTHING IN THIS CROWD.
OKAY, EVERYBODY. TIME TO GET FINDING ALL THOSE BARS AND COINS!
SO, IT'S A CHOCOLATE HUNT!
YOWCH!
AND HE SAID WE'D GET UNDER HIS FEET.
THE WORLD'S GREATEST BOY DETECTIVE DIDN'T FIND A SINGLE BAR - IT'S EMBARRASSING!
BUT, BUT...

DANDY WRESTLING ENTERTAINMENT
YOU'RE JOINING US LIVE AT GRUMBLY-ON-SEA...
...FOR A SEASIDE SLAM DOWN BETWEEN...
...BUCKET-HEAD AND BEACHBALL.
LET'S SEE HOW IT STARTED.
BUCKET-HEAD AND BEACHBALL WERE ENJOYING THEIR ANNUAL TRIP TO THE BEACH.
LOOK! A SWIMMING COMPETITION!
GRUMBLY-ON-SEA SUPER SUMMER SWIM-OFF
I'D WIN THAT EASILY. I'M THE BEST SWIMMER.
ARE NOT, I AM. I SWIM LIKE A FISH.
LIKE A FISH FINGER, YOU MEAN. I'M BEST.
I AM.
ME.
ME.
THERE'S ONLY ONE WAY TO SUSS THE SUPERIOR SWIMMER...
FIGHT!

AND BUCKET-HEAD IS STRAIGHT IN WITH A BUCKET-HEAD BARGE!
ZOOM!
RAMMING SPEED!
OOF!
WHAM!
BOING!
BUT BEACHBALL'S BELLY'S BOUNCED THE BARGING BUCKET BACKWARDS!
HE'S SPRINGING INTO ACTION!
BOING! BOING! BOING!
TAKE THAT, BUCKET BONCE!
BOING! BOING! BOING!
OOF... OOF... OOF!
HA! THE WINNER!
I DON'T WANT TO LET YOU DOWN, BUT...
UH-OH, IS BEACHBALL'S BRAGGING ALL HOT AIR?
OH NO!
POP!
THRRRRRRRRRRRRRRRRP!!!
WAAH!
LOOKS LIKE BEACHBALL'S SWIMMING LIKE A FLYING FISH NOW!
AND THERE YOU HAVE IT, FOLKS - CONCLUSIVE PROOF THAT BUCKET-HEAD IS THE BEST SWIMMER!
YEP, THINGS CERTAINLY DIDN'T GO *SWIMMINGLY* FOR BEACHBALL.
GRAND SWIMMING TROPHY
NICK BRENNAN

DESPERATE DAN
IT SURE IS GREAT TO GET AWAY FOR A HOLIDAY BREAK.
SUDDENLY . . .
RUMBLE!
GRUMBLE!
HM! THAT SOUNDS LIKE MAH GRANDSON'S TUM RUMBLING.
IT ISN'T!
TARNATION! A REEF! AH DON'T LIKE THE LOOK OF THAT AT ALL.
RUMBLE!
GRUMBLE!
THEN . . .
AAIIEEE!
CRUMP!
HM! MAH NEPHEW SEEMS TO HAVE FOUND A NICE SPOT TO STAY.
OOMPH!

PLOOP!
WAHOO! AH'M FREE!
OUCH!
WHUMP!
OW!
NICE HERE, AIN'T IT? LET'S GO EXPLORING.
HMPH!
NOT UNTIL YOU RESCUE OUR CASES. THEY FELL INTO THE SEA, SEE?
SHUCKS! NO NEED TO GET ANNOYED.
AH'LL GET EVERYTHING BACK AN' THAT'LL PUT THEM ALL IN A GOOD MOOD — AH HOPE!
THERE'S SOME OF IT — BUT IT'S BEEN OPENED!
I DID IT. WHATCHOO GONNA DO ABOUT IT?
AH WEARS THE TROUSERS ON THIS HERE SEA-BED.
ON THE SEA SHORE . . .
WHAT'S GOIN' ON?
I HOPE UNCLE DAN IS OKAY.
SECONDS LATER . . .
NO CRITTUR TANGLES WITH ME.
OOH! THIS IS NO JOB FOR AN OCTOPUS.
HA-HA! WELL DONE, UNCLE DAN.

NOW AH'LL DO A SPOT OF SUN-BATHIN' WHILE YOU RUSTLE UP SOME GRUB, AUNT AGGIE.
OKAY, DANIEL.
BUT . . .
OH, NO! THOSE MATCHES ARE WET. THEY WON'T LIGHT THE FIRE.
WE CAN COOK OVER THERE.
AND . . .
DAN'S SIZZLING! WE'LL LIVE OFF THE FAT OF THE LAND. HAW-HAW!
SOON AFTER . . .
IT SURE IS NICE HERE BUT THERE'S NOT A LOT TO DO.
SUDDENLY . . .
YEE-IPES! AH'VE GOT ANTS IN MAH PANTS!
WHAT?
EH?

THEY AIN'T ANTS. THEY'RE TURTLES.
DADA?
MAMA?
PAPA?
AH AIN'T YOUR KIN FOLK. LEAVE ME ALONE.
LATER . . .
HO-HO! DESPERATE DAN'S GOT PLENTY TO DO NOW — LOOKING AFTER THE YOUNG UNS!
AND I'VE GOT PLENTY TO DO LOOKING AFTER THE OLD UNS.
HO-HO! THIS IS THE BEST HOLIDAY WE'VE EVER HAD.
AH! THEY'RE CUTE LITTLE FELLOWS, AIN'T THEY?
THIS IS *TURTLEY* UNBELIEVABLE!

DINAH MO
HI, READERS! I'M DINAH MODISE, OR DINAH MO TO MY FRIENDS! I LOVE THINKING UP WAYS TO LOOK AFTER OUR ENVIRONMENT!
SAVE THE PLANET
EARTH IS FAB
HEY, DINAH! HAVE YOU FORGOTTEN WE'RE GOING TO THE BEACH TODAY?
THE BEACH? JUST THE JOB, MUM!
GO GREEN
IT'S LOGICAL TO BE ECO LOGICAL
DO NOT LITTER
WHY ON EARTH HAVE YOU BROUGHT THOSE SIGNS TO THE SEASIDE, SIS?
IT'S THE PERFECT PLACE TO BRING ATTENTION TO THE ENVIRONMENT, JUNIOR!
Amusements
SO...
I HOPE YOU'RE GOING TO DISPOSE OF THAT WRAPPER RESPONSIBLY!
ULP! OF COURSE!
DO NOT LITTER
SAVE THE PLANET
ICE CREAM
NICE ICE
THERE'S LOADS OF LITTER AROUND HERE! IT'S LIKE AN OBSTACLE COURSE!
LITTER
SWERVE!
TIDY IT UP, FOLKS! I'LL FIND OUT WHO'S RESPONSIBLE!
SAVE THE PLANET
PLEASE KEEP THE BEACH TIDY
I WAS HOPING FOR A REST, BUT IT NEEDS TO BE DONE!
RECYLIN
MORE LITTER? WHO'S DROPPING ALL THIS?
BURP! THAT BURGER AND POP WAS A NICE APPETISER! NOW FOR THE MAIN COURSE!
POP
IS IT TOO MUCH TO ASK YOU TO BIN YOUR RUBBISH?
PLEASE KEEP THE BEACH TIDY
YES! I LIKE MAKING A MESS JUST TO ANNOY YOU ECO-WARRIORS! HUR-HUR!

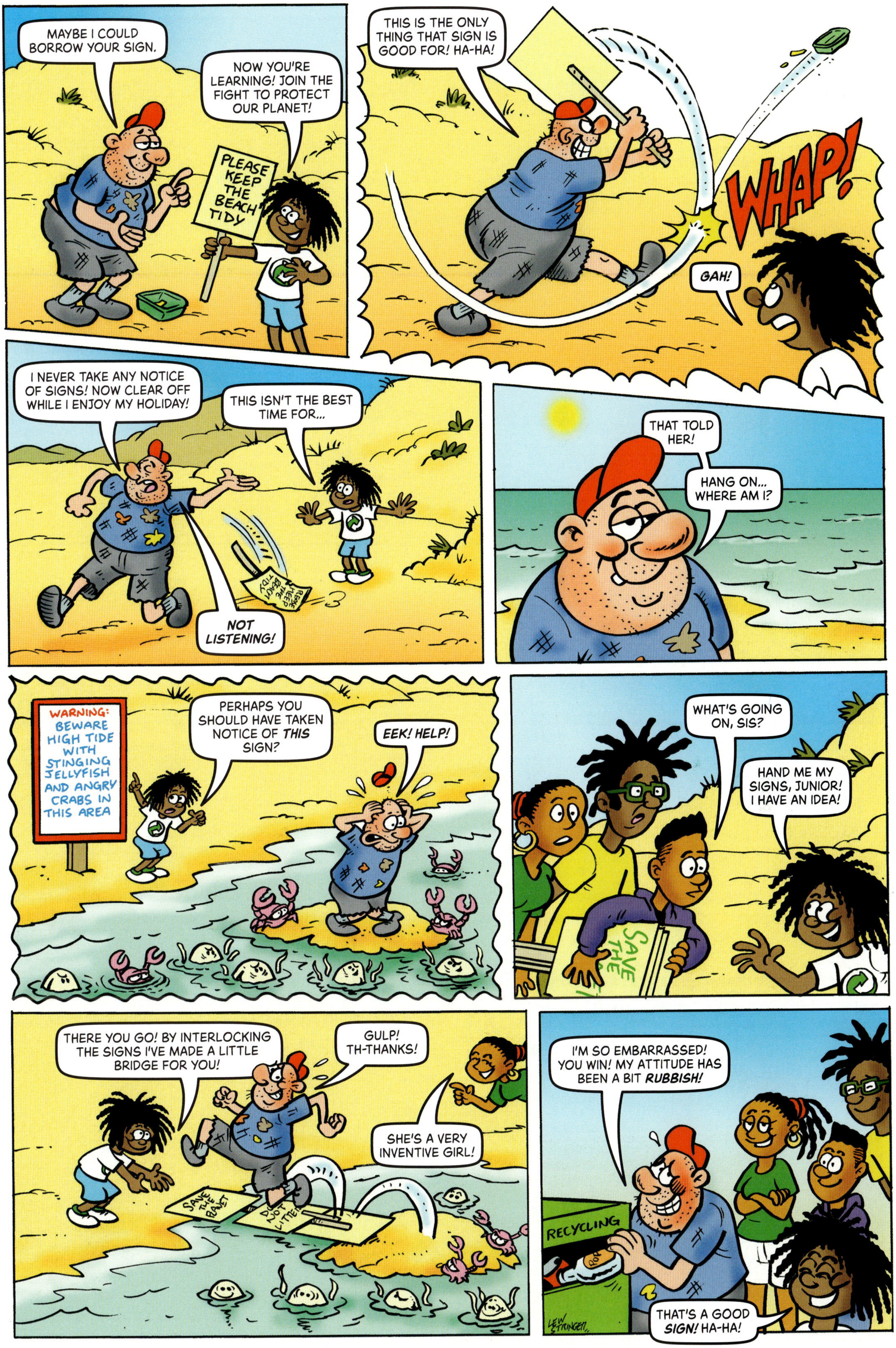
MAYBE I COULD BORROW YOUR SIGN.
NOW YOU'RE LEARNING! JOIN THE FIGHT TO PROTECT OUR PLANET!
PLEASE KEEP THE BEACH TIDY
THIS IS THE ONLY THING THAT SIGN IS GOOD FOR! HA-HA!
WHAP!
GAH!
I NEVER TAKE ANY NOTICE OF SIGNS! NOW CLEAR OFF WHILE I ENJOY MY HOLIDAY!
THIS ISN'T THE BEST TIME FOR...
NOT LISTENING!
THAT TOLD HER!
HANG ON... WHERE AM I?
WARNING: BEWARE HIGH TIDE WITH STINGING JELLYFISH AND ANGRY CRABS IN THIS AREA
PERHAPS YOU SHOULD HAVE TAKEN NOTICE OF THIS SIGN?
EEK! HELP!
WHAT'S GOING ON, SIS?
HAND ME MY SIGNS, JUNIOR! I HAVE AN IDEA!
THERE YOU GO! BY INTERLOCKING THE SIGNS I'VE MADE A LITTLE BRIDGE FOR YOU!
GULP! TH-THANKS!
SHE'S A VERY INVENTIVE GIRL!
SAVE THE PLANET
I'M SO EMBARRASSED! YOU WIN! MY ATTITUDE HAS BEEN A BIT RUBBISH!
RECYCLING
THAT'S A GOOD SIGN! HA-HA!
LEW STRINGER

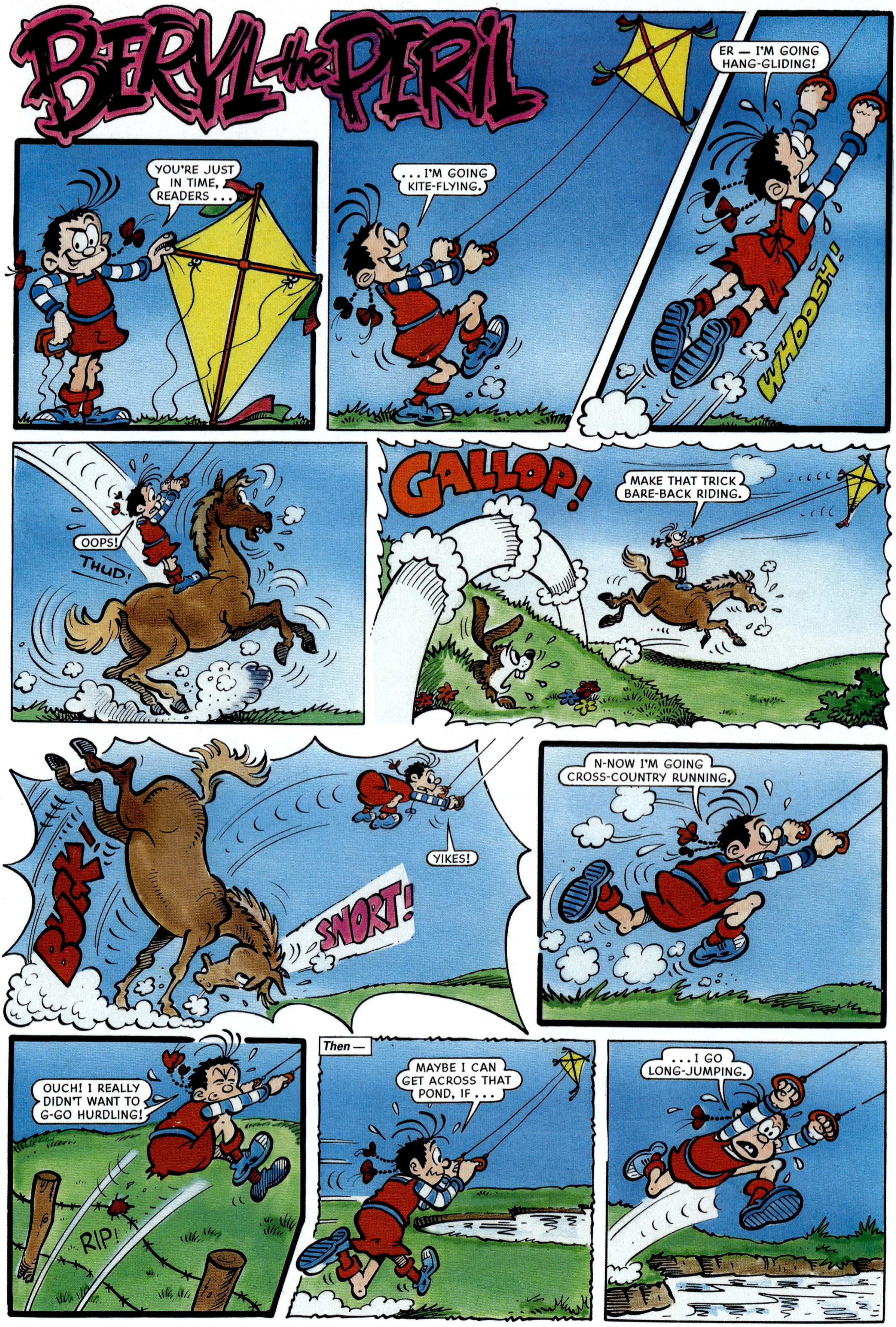
BERYL the PERIL
YOU'RE JUST IN TIME, READERS . . .
. . . I'M GOING KITE-FLYING.
ER — I'M GOING HANG-GLIDING!
WHOOSH!
OOPS!
THUD!
GALLOP!
MAKE THAT TRICK BARE-BACK RIDING.
BUCK!
YIKES!
SNORT!
N-NOW I'M GOING CROSS-COUNTRY RUNNING.
OUCH! I REALLY DIDN'T WANT TO G-GO HURDLING!
RIP!
Then —
MAYBE I CAN GET ACROSS THAT POND, IF . . .
. . . I GO LONG-JUMPING.

SPLASH!
GLUB! I DIDN'T QUITE MAKE IT . . .
. . . SO I'LL JUST GO WATER-SKIING INSTEAD.
OH, CRUMBS! I'M IN TROUBLE NOW!
NO, I'M NOT! I'M GOING MOUNTAINEERING!
BOUNCE!
SCRAPE!
OW! OW! I'M GOING SLEDGING — WITHOUT A SLEDGE!
CRASH!
OH, DEAR! I'M GOING TO COME TO A SUDDEN STOP . . .
SNAP!
SNAP!
. . . OR NOT!
I KNOW WHAT I'M GOING TO DO NOW . . .
FLUMP!
. . . I'M GOING TO GO TO BED — BLEH-H!

CORPORAL CLOTT

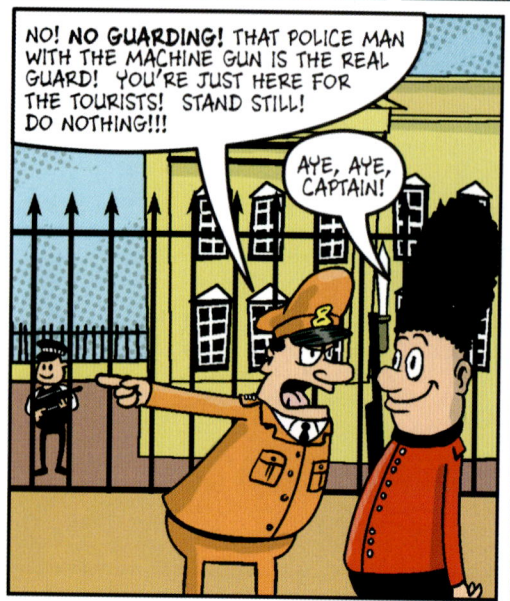

COLONEL GRUMBLY IS REGRETTING TRYING TO TEACH CLOTT HOW TO DRIVE A TANK.

GOOD GRAVY! THAT BOY CAN'T DO ANYTHING!

I THINK I KNOW WHAT I DID WRONG THAT TIME, YOUR MAJESTY!

STOP CALLING ME YOUR MAJESTY! I'M NOT **THE KING**!

OH, BUT WAIT! THAT GIVES ME AN IDEA! HA-HA-HA!

HA-HA-HA! WHY ARE WE LAUGHING?

BUCKINGHAM PALACE...

OKAY, IT'S YOUR JOB TO DO NOTHING! **NOTHING**, CLOTT! CAN YOU DO THAT? STAND STILL?

NOTHING BUT GUARD THE KING. GOT IT!

NO! **NO GUARDING!** THAT POLICE MAN WITH THE MACHINE GUN IS THE REAL GUARD! YOU'RE JUST HERE FOR THE TOURISTS! STAND STILL! DO NOTHING!!!

AYE, AYE, CAPTAIN!

JUST REMEMBER! STILL AS A STATUE!

AND I'M NOT A CAPTAIN, I'M A COLONEL!

YES, CHIEF!

EIGHT HOURS LATER...

HAD A GOOD DAY, CLOTT? MANAGED TO STAY STILL ALL DAY?

YES, YOUR LORDSHIP!

Panel 1: REALLY? ODD THAT THERE'S SOMEONE WHO LOOKS A LOT LIKE YOU ALL OVER THE INTERNET!

Panel 2: THIS IS FROM THE WATSON FAMILY'S FACEBOOK WITH THE CAPTION, "FUN AND GAMES AT THE PALACE!"

Panel 3: OH THAT? THAT WAS ONE MOMENTARY SLIP UP, YOUR WORSHIP!

Panel 4: WHAT ABOUT THIS TRENDING ON TWITTER? #CRAZYGUARD

Panel 5: AND WHO'S THAT WEARING YOUR HAT?
I CAN'T REMEMBER HER NAME. SHE WAS REALLY NICE THOUGH.

Panel 6: HERE YOU ARE GIVING OUT FREE PIGGYBACKS!

Panel 7: AND HERE'S A VIDEO OF YOU PUSHING IN LINE AT THE ICE CREAM VAN!

Panel 8: OUT OF THE WAY! THE KING WANTS A MINTY MAGNUM!
BARGE! SHOVE!

Panel 9: IT WASN'T FOR THE KING, WAS IT?
THIS HAT IS VERY, VERY HOT!

Panel 10: COME ON! WE'RE GOING BACK. WHERE'S YOUR RIFLE?
RIFLE?
I HAD A RIFLE, DID I?

Panel 11: NEARBY...
WHERE DID HE GET THAT TOY RIFLE FROM?
ARE YOU SURE IT'S A TOY?
IT'S DEFINITELY A TOY - THERE'S NO WAY THEY'D GIVE CLOTT A REAL ONE! - ED

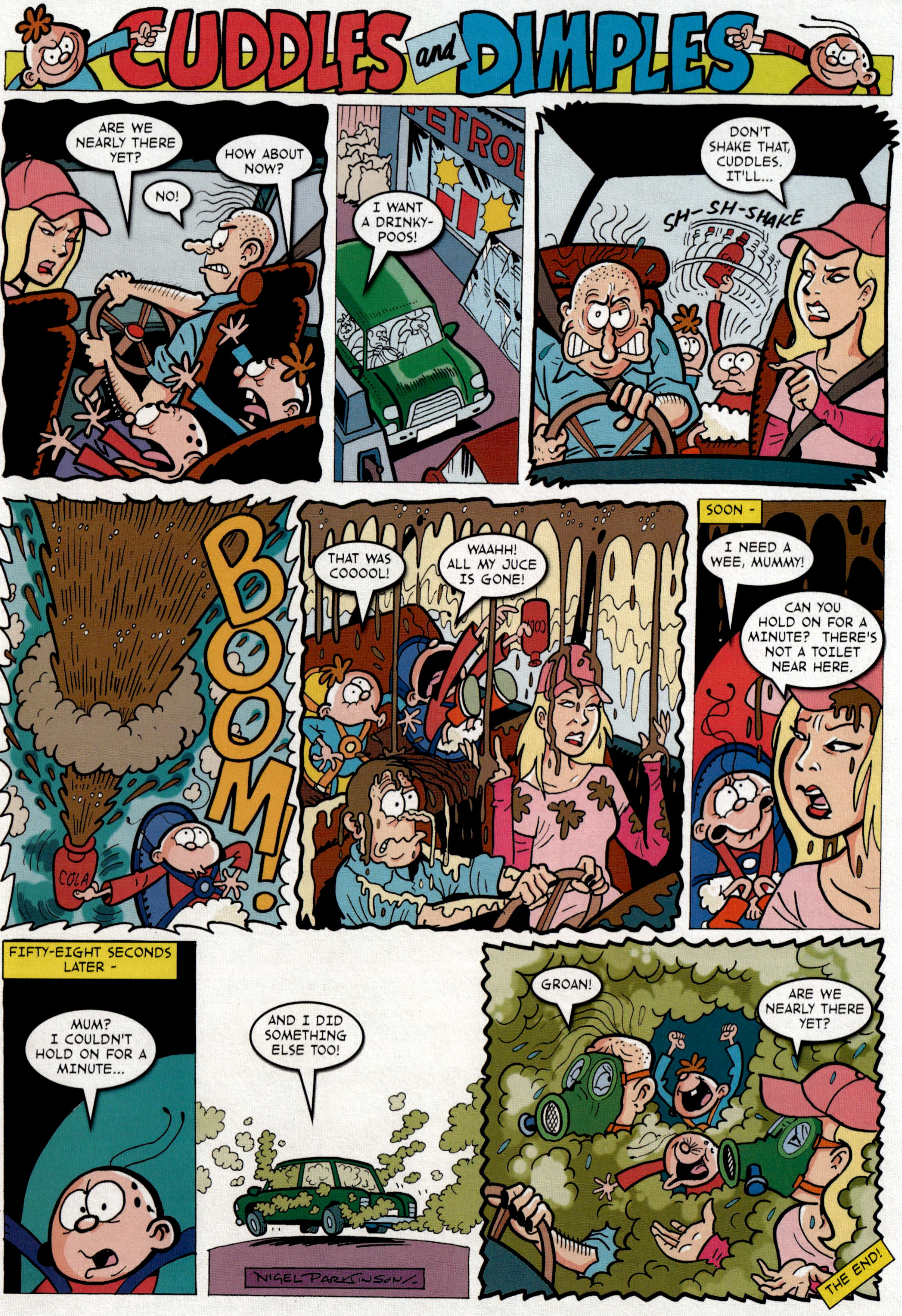
CUDDLES and DIMPLES
ARE WE NEARLY THERE YET?
NO!
HOW ABOUT NOW?
PETROL
I WANT A DRINKY-POOS!
DON'T SHAKE THAT, CUDDLES. IT'LL...
SH-SH-SHAKE
COLA
BOOM!
THAT WAS COOOOL!
WAAHH! ALL MY JUCE IS GONE!
SOON -
I NEED A WEE, MUMMY!
CAN YOU HOLD ON FOR A MINUTE? THERE'S NOT A TOILET NEAR HERE.
FIFTY-EIGHT SECONDS LATER -
MUM? I COULDN'T HOLD ON FOR A MINUTE...
AND I DID SOMETHING ELSE TOO!
NIGEL PARKINSON
GROAN!
ARE WE NEARLY THERE YET?
THE END!

HYDE & SHRIEK
DANDY
11
HO-HUMM! EVEN MORE SKINT THAN USUAL! SIGH...
EMPTY!
OINK?
I NEVER THOUGHT I'D SEE THE DAY, BUT THERE'S ONLY ONE WAY TO RAISE SOME DOSH.
WE'LL JUST HAVE TO OPEN THE CASTLE UP.
TO... (CHOKE)... TOURISTS.
GUIDED TOURS OF THE CASTLE. ONLY £5-00
STIFLED GUFFAW.
AW-PHWAW-HAW-HAWW! OH, HAR-DE-HAR-HAR!
HOOT! MOCK! HEAVE! SHAKE!
GUIDED TOURS OF THE CASTLE. ONLY £5-00
JUST WHAT IS SO FUNNY, YOUNG MASTER?
GLOWER!
SNORT! WHO'S GOING TO PAY GOOD MONEY TO LOOK ROUND THIS SMELLY OLD HEAP? GUFFAW!!
CASTLE JECKYLL
Abandon y-fronts all who enter here!
Here lies a zombie... He'd like to meet you... He'll suck out your brain and then he'll eat you!
HUMPH! YOU'LL SEE! THE TRIPPERS WILL SOON BE FLOCKING IN!!
BALEFUL GLARE!
HAW-HAW! DREAM ON, ZEPPELIN-PANTS! SNICKER!
HELPLESS MIRTH!
THREE WEEKS LATER....
HUH! NOT ONE SINGLE VISITOR!!
GUIDED TOURS OF THE CASTLE. ONLY £5-00
GUIDE
CASH
TOLD YOU! THERE'S NOTHING FOR ANYONE TO SEE IN THIS BORIN' OL' DUMP!

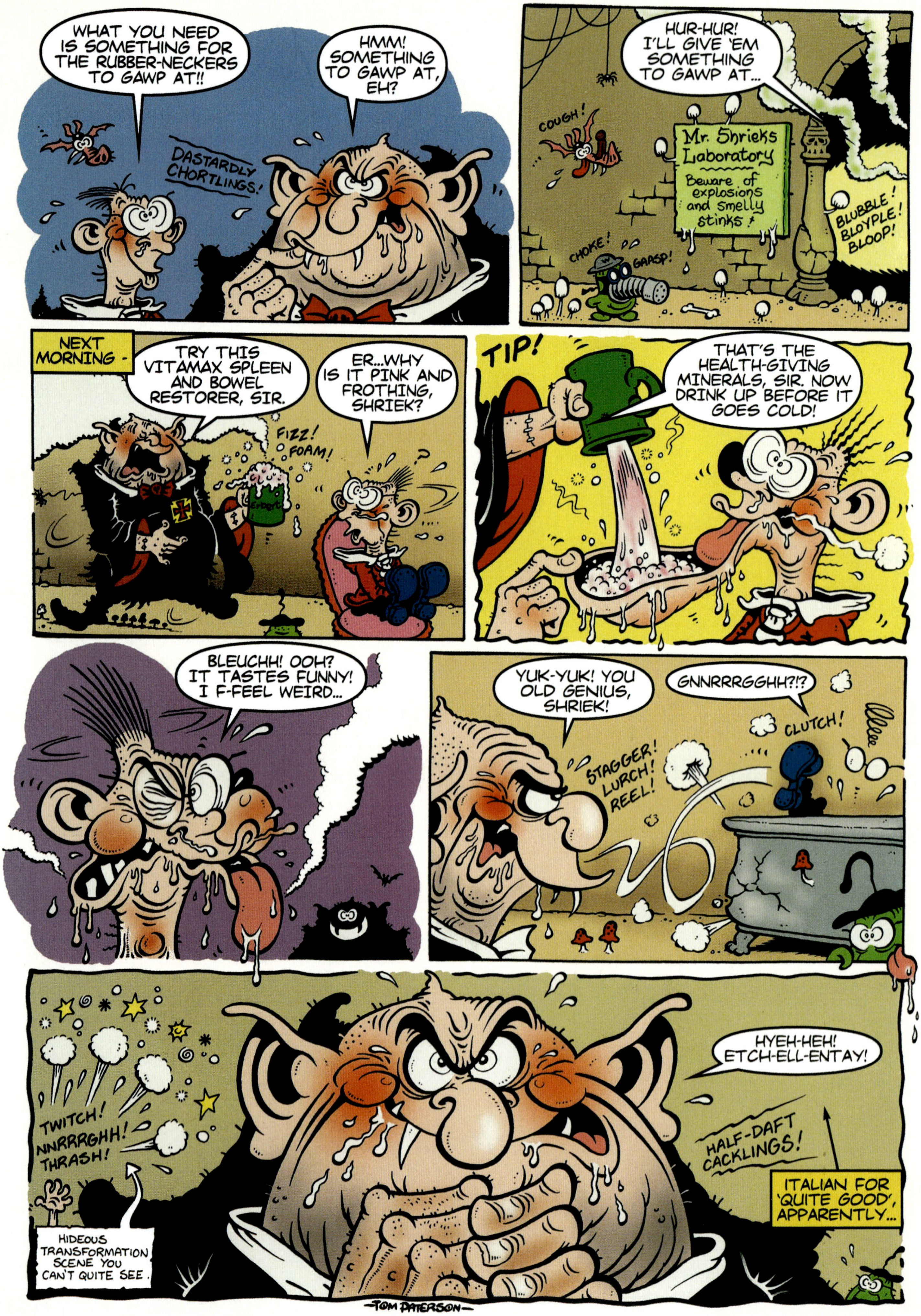

WHAT YOU NEED IS SOMETHING FOR THE RUBBER-NECKERS TO GAWP AT!!
HMM! SOMETHING TO GAWP AT, EH?
DASTARDLY CHORTLINGS!
HUR-HUR! I'LL GIVE 'EM SOMETHING TO GAWP AT...
COUGH!
Mr. Shrieks Laboratory
Beware of explosions and smelly stinks
BLUBBLE! BLOYPLE! BLOOP!
CHOKE!
GAASP!
NEXT MORNING -
TRY THIS VITAMAX SPLEEN AND BOWEL RESTORER, SIR.
ER...WHY IS IT PINK AND FROTHING, SHRIEK?
FIZZ! FOAM!
TIP!
THAT'S THE HEALTH-GIVING MINERALS, SIR. NOW DRINK UP BEFORE IT GOES COLD!
BLEUCHH! OOH? IT TASTES FUNNY! I F-FEEL WEIRD...
YUK-YUK! YOU OLD GENIUS, SHRIEK!
GNNRRRGGHH?!?
STAGGER! LURCH! REEL!
CLUTCH!
TWITCH! NNRRRGHH! THRASH!
HIDEOUS TRANSFORMATION SCENE YOU CAN'T QUITE SEE.
HYEH-HEH! ETCH-ELL-ENTAY!
HALF-DAFT CACKLINGS!
ITALIAN FOR 'QUITE GOOD', APPARENTLY...
TOM PATERSON

DREADLOCK HOLMES

Panel 1: KID DETECTIVE SUMMER CAMP! MY FAVOURITE TIME OF THE YEAR!

Sign: KID DETECTIVE SUMMER CAMP

Panel 2: I LIKE IT BECAUSE I AM OBVIOUSLY THE GREATEST DETECTIVE IN THE WHOLE CAMP!

Panel 3: I DO NOT THINK SO, MY FRIEND! FOR IT IS I, HERCULES PARROT, WHO IS THE GREATEST DETECTIVE!

Panel 4: THAT'S NOT QUITE RIGHT, IS IT, DEAR? DID YOU FORGET THAT I'M THE BEST DETECTIVE HERE? MISSY MARBLES, SIGH.

Panel 5: THE ONLY MYSTERY THAT I CAN'T SOLVE IS WHY YOU TWO THINK YOU ARE BETTER THAN ME! REALLY?

Panel 6: I'M SUCH A GREAT DETECTIVE THAT I WORKED OUT THE END OF 'THE MYSTERY OF THE LOST PEARLS' BY PAGE TEN.

Book: THE MYSTERY OF THE LOST PEARLS

Panel 7: I WORKED OUT THE END OF 'THE MYSTERIOUS DETECTIVE' BY READING THE BACK COVER.

Book: THE MYSTERIOUS DETECTIVE

Panel 8: I WORKED OUT THE END OF 'THE HOTEL OF MYSTERY' JUST BY READING THE TITLE!

Book: THE HOTEL OF MYSTERY

I SOLVED THE MYSTERY OF WHO HAD BEEN STEALING THE BISCUITS IN MY HOUSE.
IT WAS MY MUM!
I SOLVED THE MYSTERY OF WHO HAD BEEN EATING MY HOMEWORK.
IT WAS MY DOG!
I SOLVED THE MYSTERY OF WHO WAS HOARDING ALL THE MARBLES IN MY VILLAGE.
IT WAS ME!
THAT'S FUNNY BECAUSE IT SOUNDS LIKE YOU'VE LOST YOUR MARBLES!
UNLIKE YOU, I DON'T NEED TO RESORT TO INSULTS, YOU BIG SMELLYFACE!
I USE TRADITIONAL DETECTIVE TOOLS LIKE THIS MAGNIFYING GLASS!
I USE THE LATEST DETECTIVE TOOLS, LIKE SPECIAL APPS!
I USE THE BEST DETECTIVE TOOL OF ALL - MY BRAIN!
I'M THE BEST DETECTIVE!
NO, I AM!
NO, I'M THE BEST!
WHY ARE YOU THREE STILL HERE? THE CAMP ACTIVITIES HAVE ALREADY STARTED!
HUH?
YOU WERE SO BUSY ARGUING ABOUT WHO WAS THE BEST DETECTIVE YOU DIDN'T DETECT YOU WERE MISSING OUT ON ALL THE FUN!
I CAN DEDUCE THAT IT'S GOING TO BE A LONG WEEK.

DESPERATE DAN

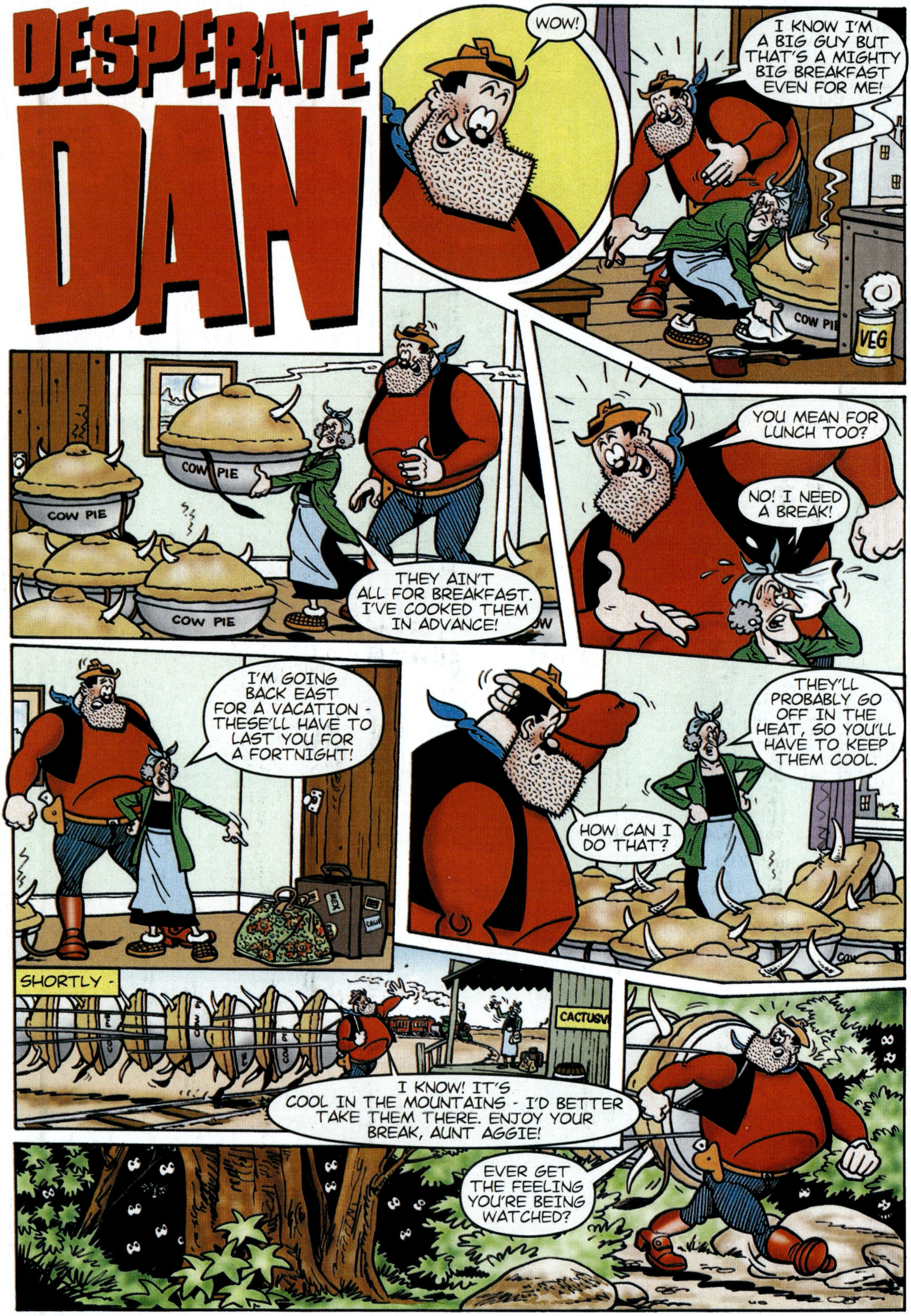